Lecture Notes in Computer Science 12594

More information about this subseries at http://www.springer.com/series/7412

Maria De Marsico · Gabriella Sanniti di Baja ·
Ana Fred (Eds.)

Pattern Recognition Applications and Methods

9th International Conference, ICPRAM 2020
Valletta, Malta, February 22–24, 2020
Revised Selected Papers

 Springer

Editors
Maria De Marsico
Sapienza Università di Roma
Roma, Italy

Ana Fred
Instituto de Telecomunicações
Lisbon, Portugal

University of Lisbon
Lisbon, Portugal

Gabriella Sanniti di Baja
ICAR
Consiglio Nazionale delle Ricerche
Naples, Napoli, Italy

ISSN 0302-9743   ISSN 1611-3349 (electronic)
Lecture Notes in Computer Science
ISBN 978-3-030-66124-3   ISBN 978-3-030-66125-0 (eBook)
https://doi.org/10.1007/978-3-030-66125-0

LNCS Sublibrary: SL6 – Image Processing, Computer Vision, Pattern Recognition, and Graphics

This Springer imprint is published by the registered company Springer Nature Switzerland AG
The registered company address is: Gewerbestrasse 11, 6330 Cham, Switzerland

Preface

This book includes the extended and revised versions of a set of selected papers from the 9th International Conference on Pattern Recognition Applications and Methods (ICPRAM 2020), held in Valletta, Malta, during February 22–24, 2020.

ICPRAM is a major point of contact between researchers, engineers, and practitioners on the areas of pattern recognition and machine learning, both from theoretical and application perspectives. Contributions describing applications of pattern recognition techniques to real-world problems, interdisciplinary research, experimental, and/or theoretical studies yielding new insights that advance pattern recognition methods are especially encouraged.

ICPRAM 2020 received 102 paper submissions from 33 countries, of which the seven papers in this book constitute the 7%. The seven papers were selected by the event chairs and their selection was based on a number of criteria that include the classifications and comments provided by the Program Committee members, the session chairs' assessment, and also the program chairs' global view of all papers included in the technical program. The authors of the selected papers were then invited to submit a revised and extended version of their papers, having at least 30% innovative material.

The first four papers in the book are in the applications area, while the remaining three papers are in the theory and methods area.

In the first paper, the authors face the problem of building a universal classifier for traffic sign recognition. The classifier has to deal with large intra-class variations in the classes and also similarities among various sign classes. Authors use attention network for country independent classification. The new building block architecture shows significant improvement of classification accuracy with respect to building block architecture (VGG) used in a previous paper.

In the second paper, multi-object tracking and segmentation (MOTS) of moving objects in traffic video datasets are considered. A novel method for tracking multiple objects (MaskADNet) is proposed, which uses masked images as input for training ADNet. The segmentation masks obtained after tracking using MaskADNet have a better Jaccard index or Intersection over Union for masks.

The third paper deals with emotion recognition (ER). Authors discuss methods for analyzing the non-linguistic component of vocalized speech and propose a method for producing lower dimensional representations of sound spectrograms that respect their temporal structure.

By taking into account that most modern day consumer cameras are affected by some level of radial distortion, which must be compensated for in order to get accurate estimates, authors of the fourth paper propose a novel polynomial solver for radially distorted planar motion compatible homographies. The suggested algorithm is shown to work well inside a RANSAC loop on both synthetic and real data.

In the fifth paper, data acquired in a natural mixed forest by means of an unmanned aerial vehicle are considered. A suitable pre-processing step is introduced after which six common clustering algorithms are used to detect tree tops and five different deep learning architectures are employed to classify tree tops depending on the degree of affectation due to a parasite infestation. Classification results reach error rates as low as 0.096.

The sixth paper deals with deep neural networks (DNNs) and investigates how to reduce model complexity – without performance degradation – by pruning useless connections. Authors try to answer the question of "how similar are representations in pruned and unpruned models?" and show that the results depend critically on the used similarity measure.

Finally, in the last paper, the authors analyze multiple approaches in indefinite learning and suggest a novel, efficient preprocessing operation which widely preserves the domain-specific information, while still providing a Mercer kernel function. In particular, we address practical aspects like a out of sample extension and an effective implementation of the approach. An extensive experimental work is done on various typical data sets obtaining superior results in the field.

We would like to thank all the authors for their contributions and also the reviewers who helped ensure the quality of this publication.

February 2020

Maria De Marsico
Gabriella Sanniti di Baja
Ana Fred

Organization

Conference Chair

Ana Fred   Instituto de Telecomunicações and University
                                        of Lisbon, Portugal

Program Co-chairs

Maria De Marsico   Sapienza Università di Roma, Italy
Gabriella Sanniti di Baja   CNR, Italy

Program Committee

Andrea Abate   University of Salerno, Italy
Ashraf AbdelRaouf   Misr International University (MIU), Egypt
Rahib Abiyev   Near East University, Turkey
Lale Akarun   Bogazici University, Turkey
Mayer Aladjem   Ben-Gurion University of the Negev, Israel
Rocío Alaiz-Rodríguez   Universidad de León, Spain
Mahmood Azimi-Sadjadi   Colorado State University, USA
Silvio Barra   University of Cagliari, Italy
Stefano Berretti   University of Florence, Italy
Monica Bianchini   University of Siena, Italy
Isabelle Bloch   Télécom ParisTech, Université Paris-Saclay, France
Andrea Bottino   Politecnico di Torino, Italy
Paula Brito   Universidade do Porto, Portugal
Fabian Bürger   Valeo Vision, France
Marinella Cadoni   Università degli Studi di Sassari, Italy
Javier Calpe   Universitat de València, Spain
Virginio Cantoni   Università degli Studi di Pavia, Italy
Guillaume Caron   Université de Picardie Jules Verne, France
Rama Chellappa   University of Maryland, USA
Sergio Cruces   Universidad de Sevilla, Spain
Rozenn Dahyot   Trinity College Dublin, Ireland
Luiza de Macedo Mourelle   State University of Rio de Janeiro, Brazil
Yago Diez   Yamagata University, Japan
Jean-Louis Dillenseger   Université de Rennes 1, France
Duane Edgington   Monterey Bay Aquarium Research Institue, USA
Kjersti Engan   University of Stavanger, Norway
Haluk Eren   Firat University, Turkey
Giorgio Fumera   University of Cagliari, Italy
Vicente Garcia   Autonomous University of Ciudad Juárez, Mexico

Friedhelm Schwenker	University of Ulm, Germany
Humberto Sossa	Instituto Politécnico Nacional-CIC, Mexico
Tania Stathaki	Imperial College London, UK
Mu-Chun Su	National Central University, Taiwan, China
Eulalia Szmidt	Systems Research Institute, Polish Academy of Sciences, Poland
Monique Thonnat	Inria, France
Ricardo Torres	Norwegian University of Science and Technology (NTNU), Norway
Genny Tortora	Università degli Studi di Salerno, Italy
Edmondo Trentin	Università degli Studi di Siena, Italy
Rosa Valdovinos Rosas	Universidad Autonoma del Estado de Mexico, Mexico
Ernest Valveny	Universitat Autònoma de Barcelona, Spain
Sebastiano Vascon	Ca'Foscari University, Italy
Sebastian Ventura	University of Cordoba, Spain
Antanas Verikas	Halmstad University, Sweden
Panayiotis Vlamos	Ionian University, Greece
Asmir Vodencarevic	Siemens Healthcare GmbH, Germany
Laurent Wendling	LIPADE, France
Slawomir Wierzchon	Polish Academy of Sciences, Poland
Richard Wilson	University of York, UK
Shengkun Xie	Ryerson University, Canada
Jing-Hao Xue	University College London, UK
Chan-Yun Yang	National Taipei University, Taiwan, China
Yusuf Yaslan	Istanbul Technical University, Turkey
Slawomir Zadrozny	Polish Academy of Sciences, Poland
Pavel Zemcik	Brno University of Technology, Czech Republic
Bob Zhang	University of Macau, Macau, China
Reyer Zwiggelaar	Aberystwyth University, UK

Additional Reviewers

Qiqi Bao	Tsinghua University, China
As Mansur	Kyushu University, Japan
Eduardo Pérez	University of Cordoba, Spain
Lorenzo Putzu	University of Cagliari, Italy

Invited Speakers

Andrea Cavallaro	Queen Mary University of London, UK
Cristina Conati	University of British Columbia, Canada
Max Welling	University of Amsterdam, The Netherlands

Contents

End to End Deep Neural Network Classifier Design for Universal Sign Recognition

Vartika Sengar[1]([⊠]), Renu M. Rameshan[1], and Senthil Ponkumar[2]

[1] School of Computing and Engineering, Indian Institute of Technology, Mandi, Himachal Pradesh, India
vartika.sengar@gmail.com, renumr@iitmandi.ac.in
[2] Continental Automotive Components (India) Pvt. Ltd., Bengaluru, India
senthil.ponkumar@continental-corporation.com

Abstract. Self-driving cars and Advanced Driver Assistance Systems rely heavily on Traffic Sign Recognition for safe maneuvering on the roads. But traffic signs can vary from one country to another, thereby necessitating multiple classifiers or a single universal classifier which can handle variations across countries. This paper reports our attempt at building a universal classifier. This classifier has to deal with large intra-class variations in the classes and also similarities among various difficult to distinguish traffic sign classes. This paper is an extension of our previous work in which we proposed a hierarchical classifier for traffic signs of a specific country. In hierarchical classification, dedicated classifiers are trained for classes which are more difficult to distinguish. Such similar classes are grouped together automatically by learning category hierarchy from the confusion matrix of a flat classifier (building block). In this paper, we use attention network for country independent classification. Here, CNN itself pays attention to regions in an image which are more discriminative and thus results in better classification for such problems. The aim here is to design a traffic sign recognition framework which can be used for multiple countries and be able to classify even the hard to distinguish classes by exploiting category hierarchy of traffic signs. The model is evaluated on traffic signs of seven countries namely Belgium, China, Croatia, Russia, Spain, Germany and Italy. The new building block architecture shows significant improvement of classification accuracy that is 97.7% as compared to building block architecture (VGG) used in our previous paper that is 95.1%.

Keywords: Hierarchical classification · Machine learning · Feedforward neural networks · Data processing · Clustering methods · Image processing · Pattern recognition · Feature extraction · Attention networks · Convolutional neural networks

© Springer Nature Switzerland AG 2020
M. De Marsico et al. (Eds.): ICPRAM 2020, LNCS 12594, pp. 1–12, 2020.
https://doi.org/10.1007/978-3-030-66125-0_1

1   Introduction

Traffic sign classification is a challenging task as it has to deal with traffic signs belonging to different countries having different number of traffic sign categories. Figure 1 shows three signs. Figure 1(a) and Fig. 1(b) shows signs of same class which are visually different. Whereas, Fig. 1(c) shows a sign from a different class which is visually similar to the sign class of Fig. 1(a) and Fig. 1(b). Referring to this figure, the first major challenge is revealed as large intra-class variation and small inter-class variability.

(a) STOP sign   (b) STOP sign   (c) DO NOT ENTER sign

Fig. 1. Example showing large intra-class variation and small inter-class variability.

As described in our earlier paper [1], in sign classification visual separability among the classes is not equal. As shown in Fig. 2, some sign categories are more difficult to differentiate than others and some are very alike. Figure 2(a) shows signs which are visually different and thus can easily be classified whereas Fig. 2(b) shows signs which are very similar and difficult to discriminate. Thus, dedicated classifiers are needed to classify difficult to differentiate sign classes. To have better recognition, keen observation is required in manually grouping different sign classes. Its analysis is time consuming and at times error prone too. Automating the classification of sign classes guided by machine learning is efficiently handled by a hierarchical classifier [1] which is capable enough to make the effortless inclusion of the new category of signboards.

(a) Easy to differentiate classes

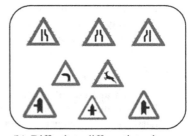

(b) Difficult to differentiate classes

Fig. 2. Examples of easy and difficult traffic sign classes.

A well designed traffic sign recognition system should not only perform well on signs of a particular country but it should also be able to properly recognize the signs of other countries, handling all the possible variations of a particular category in a country. In this work, the goal is to design a scalable universal machine learning based approach which can efficiently take care of wide intra-class variations without extracting desired handcrafted features beforehand. Here scalable means adapting to class level changes and database changes.

The above discussion brings out the necessity for a hierarchical classifier as well as a universal classifier which is country independent in the scope of traffic sign recognition, as shown in Fig. 3.

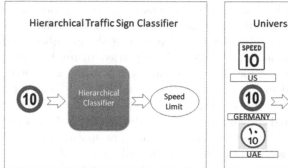 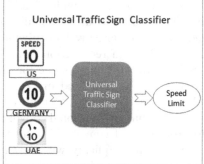

Fig. 3. Need for both hierarchical and universal classifier.

The earlier work [1] solves the problem of classification for one country; the problem of a single classifier which is invariant to country specific changes is still not solved. In human perspective, there may be a slight variation in each class sign as we move from one country to another. But for a machine to handle such variations may be confusing. The existing solutions in literature work for two [3] or three countries [4] only. Convolution network based solutions can be thought of for designing a single architecture which can be used for multiple countries, thereby eliminating the need for country-specific classifiers. Key to such solutions is learning CNN parameters such that the features obtained are discriminative. One way of doing this is by using triplet loss function for getting embeddings such that the embeddings of images of the same class lies closer to each other and are distant from the embeddings of images from other classes [7]. These embeddings lie on a manifold and any distance measure in manifold can be used for classification. Other loss functions can also be used which imposes a margin between images belonging to one class. Also, techniques which are used to improve the mid-level learning capabilities of CNN by paying attention to the discriminative regions in an image can be used to solve this problem which is similar to fine-grained image classification problem.

In this paper we propose a solution to classify traffic signs from multiple countries. For this we collected traffic sign images from seven countries, namely,

Belgium [18], China [19], Croatia [20], Russia [21], Spain [22], Germany [23] and Italy [24]. We modified our base network or building block from VGG8 to an attention based network which shows reasonable performance on data from the seven countries.

The paper is organized as follows. Section 2 describes review of related literature. Section 3 explains the method for designing universal hierarchical classifier. The experimentation details along with results are presented in Sect. 4. Conclusions and future work is discussed in Sect. 5.

2   Related Work

The idea of designing a single classifier for universal sign recognition greatly reduces the need for country-specific classifiers. Thus, a single self-driving car trained only once can travel worldwide without switching the classifiers. Some works in traffic sign recognition domain have already tried to implement this idea. Saha et al. [3] proposes one for all architecture which works well for multiple datasets. The idea used in [3] is of dilated residual learning. The dilated convolutions are used whose effective receptive field grows exponentially, which is much quicker than conventional convolution, without the loss of resolution which results from strided convolution and pooling. This merges spatial information across inputs more quickly with fewer layers. In [3], dilated residual learning is used which joins residual convolution blocks with hierarchical dilated skip connections. This model is trained and tested on German Traffic Sign Benchmark (GTSRB) [23] and Belgium Traffic Sign Benchmark (BTSC) [18]. Another work on multiple-dataset traffic sign classification using single CNN is described by JuriÅi et al. [4]. A single deep CNN model is used which is trained with dropout. This performs well on intersection and union of three different country datasets namely Germany, Belgium, and Croatia. A multi-scale architecture is described in [4]. Here, the branch-offs from the convolutional layers are concatenated after adding fully connected layer on top of each convolution-pooling block. This multi-scale architecture helps to extract several abstract features per scale before combining in fully connected layers. Also, Rosario et al. [5] explains transfer learning techniques to use the knowledge gained from an already developed model of a specific country to better recognize traffic signs from another country. In [6] Yang et al. explains efficient traffic sign recognition system with scale aware CNN consisting of a classification module which fuses multi-scale and multi-level features followed by a fully connected and softmax layer.

In addition there are certain loss functions in literature which can be used to maximize the inter-class variance and minimize intra-class variance. These introduce a margin between positive example to all other negative examples. Triplet Loss [7], Large margin Softmax Loss [8], Angular Softmax Loss [9], Contrastive Center Loss [10], Large Margin Cosine Loss [11] and Additive Margin Softmax Loss [12] all share the same idea of increasing the discriminative power of features. Yang et al. [13] explains convolution prototype learning where prototype loss is introduced to provide intra-class compactness of feature representation.

Another category of solutions which can possibly solve the universal sign recognition problem is by attending the most discriminative regions during classification, thereby increasing the accuracy for difficult fine-grained classification problems. Valev et al. [14] compares the performance of various recent deep learning architectures like VGG, ResNet, Inception, DenseNet and MobileNet for fine-grained vehicle classification. In [14] it is concluded that DenseNet proves to be the best among all architectures for classification after fine tuning weights of the pre-trained network because every layer is connected to every other layer which preserve information of both input and skipped layers. Yang et al. [15] describes a collaborative learning scheme which includes multi-agents. In this network three agents are used:

- Navigator which proposes the most discriminative region.
- Teacher who evaluates the region proposed by navigator and gives feedback.
- Scrutinizer who inspects proposed regions from Navigator and do classification.

Wang et al. [16] proposes a feedforward CNN architecture which is formed by stacking multiple attention modules. Each module consists of a mask branch and a trunk branch. Trunk branch is a normal feature processing branch. Mask branch is used to learn different attention mask for different levels. The attention is not restricted to a fixed location but to different locations in a single image. Attention mask softly weights the input image feature by suppressing bad features and enhancing good discriminative features. Similarly, Fu et al. in [17] proposed a recurrent attention proposal subnetwork. This network learns discriminative attention region and its feature representation at multiple scales. At each scale there are two subnetworks - classification subnetwork and attention proposal network. Attention proposal network proposes attention region for next scale iteratively from coarse to a finer level of attention. Two loss functions are used, one for intra-scale classification loss and another for inter scale ranking loss. Optimization is done in an alternating manner. For solving fine grained classification problem, Wang et al. in [2] focuses on discriminative patches in input image not by using any auxiliary network or feature encoding but by learning 1×1 filter bank which acts as discriminative patch detectors. This is claimed to be better than the previous approach of localization because here there is no trade-off between localization and recognition. In [17] and other similar works, initially the corresponding parts are determined which motivates similarity between the parts followed by comparison of appearance of these parts to identify the discriminative information which motivates dissimilarity amongst the parts across classes. Thus, there always exists a trade-off. In [2], there is no such trade-off and discriminative patches are not necessarily shared across classes. Therefore, full focus is on classification. In our work we applied the idea of learning 1×1 discriminative filter bank from [2] to our building block [1] to solve the problem of a universal classifier for traffic signs recognition.

3   Methodology

The idea is to modify the building block net of previously proposed hierarchical classifier architecture to learn convolutional filter bank which can capture class specific discriminative patch for enhancing previous classifier to distinguish between traffic sign from multiple countries. The modification is by
adding attention mechanism of [2] where attention module was used to solve
fine grained classification problem on CUB-200-2011, Stanford Cars and FGVC-
Aircraft datasets. 1×1 convolution filter acts as a patch detector in the input
image [2]. The aim is to learn these 1×1 convolution filters which have a high
response in the discriminative region. The exemplar illustration is given in Fig. 4.

The building block architecture which was used in earlier work is shown
in Table 1 [1]. Because we need a highly localized discriminative region, small
patches or small receptive field of input feature map should be used. The receptive field is region in input image that is influenced by a particular CNN filter. It
is calculated using Eq. 1 where jump is distance between two adjacent features.

$$ReceptiveField = PreviousReceptiveField + (Kernelsize-1) * previousjump \tag{1}$$

Also, for accurate patch location, stride between the adjacent patches should be
small. The modified architecture is shown in Fig. 5.

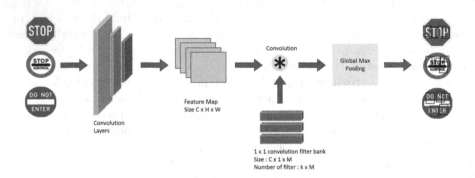

Fig. 4. 1×1 Convolution filter bank act as patch detector.

The modified architecture is structured as a two-stream asymmetric architecture. The two streams are [2]:

1. Discriminative patch branch - Classification on the basis of responses of discriminative patches.
2. Global feature branch - Classification on the basis of global feature and
appearance.

To ensure discriminative representation, the network is trained in such a
way that the patch detectors (bank of convolution filters) identify patches from

Table 1. Building block architecture details.

Layer	Configuration		Receptive field
Conv1 block	Convolution	32, 3 × 3 filters	3
	Convolution	32, 3 × 3 filters	5
	Max pooling	2 × 2	6
	Dropout	0.2	
Conv2 block	Convolution	64, 3 × 3 filters	10
	Convolution	64, 3 × 3 filters	14
	Max pooling	2 × 2	16
	Dropout	0.2	
Conv3 block	Convolution	128, 3 × 3 filters	24
	Convolution	128, 3 × 3 filters	32
	Max pooling	2 × 2	36
	Dropout	0.2	
	Flatten		
	Dense	512	
	Dropout	0.2	
	Dense	No. of classes (M)	

the discriminative regions of the image. The learning mechanism is by using convolution filter supervision which ensures direct supervision of 1×1 filters shown as the side branch in Fig. 5. If there are M classes and each class has k discriminative patches then the total number of 1×1 convolution filters needed is kM. After taking the maximum response of each convolution filter we get a kM-tuple, where each class is represented by a k-tuple. Cross-channel pooling (each value picked from one filter corresponds to one channel) is done by averaging over each group of k-tuples, thereby leading to an M-tuple, with each entry corresponding to a class. Following this, softmax is applied. The filters

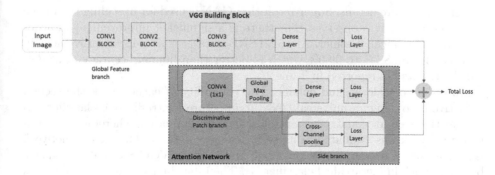

Fig. 5. Architecture of modified VGG network.

corresponding to each class finds discriminative patches from training data of that class such that the average filter response is high.

The patch detector layer initialization is done as follows. The convolution features from the pre-trained model (VGG) are extracted. At each location of the feature map, $L \times W \times C$, the energy (ℓ_2 norm of the C-tuple) is calculated. Those locations which have energy larger than the threshold are selected. The selection is done using non-max suppression with a small threshold. K-means is then applied to selected C-tuple within the class i. Cluster centers are used as initialization for filters from the class i. In this way, mid-level learning capability of CNN is enhanced.

4   Experimentation and Results

In previous work [1], the experiments were performed using dataset of single country. We used GTSRB dataset to solve classification problem of uneven visual variability of traffic signs using a deep learning based hierarchical classification design. The difficult classes were distinguished using dedicated fine category classifiers. The final prediction was the probabilistic weighted average of fine category prediction, weighted by coarse classifier prediction. The category hierarchy was learned using spectral clustering on the confusion matrix of building block CNN. For 29 class problem, the accuracy improved from 92.1% for the flat classifier to 93.3% for the hierarchical classifier. But the Top-1 accuracy of 93.3% can still be improved. To proceed in that direction the results obtained were analyzed. Two major issues which were noticed are outliers and size of images. Outliers (images which do not contain any sign) were removed statistically by fixing an upper and lower threshold on aspect ratio using box plot. This threshold entirely depends on the dataset. The second major problem which was observed is the size of the image which varies from 1×4 pixels to 108×89 pixels. The images which are very small does not contain any information in just a few pixels. This problem can be solved by removal of such small images. The accuracy obtained after removing both outliers and small sized images is 97.5%. Another issue was that upscaling by interpolation leads to loss of quality and adds blur. So, super-resolution seems to be a better option for upscaling while preserving texture details. Super-resolution GAN is used for upscaling the image by a factor of 4. It is observed that there is a significant improvement in accuracy by hierarchical classifier. Also, GTSRB dataset is showing improvement in accuracy from 98.7% to 99.0% which is better than human accuracy of 98.8%. All the results are reported in Table 2.

In order to scale up and enhance the capability of earlier work the second objective is to design a universal CNN architecture for traffic sign classification so that the need for country-specific classifiers is eliminated. Therefore, the proposed network was evaluated using seven country dataset. The VGG-8 network is used as a base network in the proposed architecture. VGG-8 was also used as a building block in hierarchical classifier [1]. The input image size for the network is $224 \times 224 \times 3$. Training is done for 300 epochs with a batch size of 14 images.

The test batch size is fixed at 64. Figure 6 shows the location of discriminative patches before and after training on some test examples from Speed Limit 20 traffic sign class.

Fig. 6. Result showing the location of attention patches before and after training for GTSRB dataset.

After the training, attention patches are more focused on the discriminative locations. As observed from the Speed Limit sign classes, the discriminative region is number written on the sign. For example, among speed limit 20, 30, 50, 60 etc., the discriminative region is 2, 3, 5, 6 respectively. This is justified from Fig. 6, as the patches after training are located over the number 2 for speed limit 20 sign class. Thus, this network can be used to locate discriminative parts when the image has lots of variation within class.

The model is trained and tested using multiple country dataset. The multiple country dataset is obtained from traffic sign dataset of seven countries- Belgium, China, Croatia, Russia, Spain, Germany and Italy. All sign classes from GTSRB is picked and all equivalent classes for the other countries are also selected to form the dataset. The resulting top-1 testing accuracy is 97.72%. The flat VGG-8 network gives top-1 testing accuracy of 95.13% which is lower than accuracy obtained using discriminative filter bank architecture. From To the best of our knowledge, this is the first such work on seven country dataset. Thus, network works well on multiple country dataset as well. The result is shown in Table 2.

Table 2. Results of experimentation done on seven countries dataset. HC: hierarchical classifier.

Dataset	Network	Accuracy	Network	Accuracy
29-Triangular: original [1]	VGG-8	92.1%	HC	93.3%
29-Triangular: outliers removed [1]	VGG-8	92.4%	HC	93.8%
29-Triangular: small size removed [1]	VGG-8	96.1%	HC	96.9%
29-Triangular: both removed [1]	VGG-8	96.7%	HC	97.5%
29-super-resolved Triangular [1]	VGG-8	95.0%	HC	97.3%
GTSRB [1]	VGG-8	98.7%	HC	99%
Seven countries traffic sign	VGG-8	95.1%	Proposed	**97.7%**

5   Conclusion and Future Work

Attention network based architecture shows improvement over our base model as used in our previous work on deep learning based hierarchical classification design. Using this more generalized universal CNN architecture for traffic sign classification we can eliminate country specific classifiers. This model can be integrated as a building block in hierarchical classifier architecture, which can enhance mid-level learning capability of CNN by using 1×1 filter as patch detectors and training it in such a manner that gives maximum response on the most discriminative regions of the image. It may result in some improvement in accuracy. We have seen that if the base model accuracy is high, the hierarchical classifier doesn't give much improvement (On GTSRB dataset: base model 98.7% and hierarchical classifier: 99.0%) [1]. The accuracy obtained on the seven countries combined data is 97.72% which is higher than accuracy obtained by VGG-8 architecture that is 95.13%. This shows that the attention model works well for multiple country traffic sign recognition. We expect the attention based VGG-8 model to provide some improvement when used with hierarchical classifiers. Pre-processing techniques and augmentation can also be applied to improve the performance especially in case when very less examples of the particular class are available.

References

1. Sengar, V., Rameshan, R.M., Ponkumar, S.: Hierarchical traffic sign recognition for autonomous driving. In: International Conference on Pattern Recognition Applications and Methods (ICPRAM), February 2020
2. Wang, Y., Morariu, V.I., Davis, L.S.: Learning a discriminative filter bank within a cnn for fine-grained recognition. In: The IEEE Conference on Computer Vision and Pattern Recognition (CVPR), June 2018
3. Saha, S., Amit Kamran, S., Shihab Sabbir, A.: Total recall: understanding traffic signs using deep convolutional neural network. In: 2018 21st International Conference of Computer and Information Technology (ICCIT), pp. 1–6, December 2018

4. JuriÅi, F., Filkovi, I., Kalafati, Z.: Multiple-dataset traffic sign classification with one CNN. In: 2015 3rd IAPR Asian Conference on Pattern Recognition (ACPR), pp. 614–618, November 2015
5. Rosario, G., Sonderman, T., Zhu, X.: Deep transfer learning for traffic sign recognition. In: 2018 IEEE International Conference on Information Reuse and Integration (IRI), pp. 178–185, July 2018
6. Yang, Y., Liu, S., Ma, W., Wang, Q., Liu, Z.: Efficient traffic-sign recognition with scale-aware CNN. CoRR, vol. abs/1805.12289 (2018)
7. Schroff, F., Kalenichenko, D., Philbin, J.: Facenet: a unified embedding for face recognition and clustering. In: 2015 IEEE Conference on Computer Vision and Pattern Recognition (CVPR), pp. 815–823, June 2015
8. Liu, W., Wen, Y., Yu, Z., Yang, M.: Large-margin softmax loss for convolutional neural networks. In: Proceedings of the 33rd International Conference on International72 Conference on Machine Learning, ICML 2016, vol. 48, pp. 507–516. JMLR.org (2016)
9. Liu, W., Wen, Y., Yu, Z., Li, M., Raj, B., Song, L.: Sphereface: deep hypersphere embedding for face recognition. In: 2017 IEEE Conference on Computer Vision and Pattern Recognition (CVPR), pp. 6738–6746, July 2017
10. Qi, C., Su, F.: Contrastive-center loss for deep neural networks. In: in 2017 IEEE International Conference on Image Processing (ICIP), pp. 2851–2855, September 2017
11. Wang, H., et al.: Cosface: large margin cosine loss for deep face recognition. In: 2018 IEEE/CVF Conference on Computer Vision and Pattern Recognition, pp. 5265–5274, June 2018
12. Wang, F., Cheng, J., Liu, W., Liu, H.: Additive margin softmax for face verification. IEEE Signal Process. Lett. **25**, 926–930 (2018)
13. Yang, H., Zhang, X., Yin, F., Liu, C.: Robust classification with convolutional prototype learning. In: 2018 IEEE/CVF Conference on Computer Vision and Pattern Recognition, pp. 3474–3482, June 2018
14. Valev, K., Schumann, A., Sommer, L.W., Beyerer, J.: A systematic evaluation of recent deep learning architectures for fine-grained vehicle classification. CoRR, vol. abs/1806.02987 (2018)
15. Yang, Z., Luo, T., Wang, D., Hu, Z., Gao, J., Wang, L.: Learning to navigate for fine-grained classification. In: Ferrari, V., Hebert, M., Sminchisescu, C., Weiss, Y. (eds.) ECCV 2018, Part XIV. LNCS, vol. 11218, pp. 438–454. Springer, Cham (2018). https://doi.org/10.1007/978-3-030-01264-9_26
16. Wang, F., et al.: Residual attention network for image classification. In: 2017 IEEE Conference on Computer Vision and Pattern Recognition (CVPR), pp. 6450–6458, July 2017
17. Fu, J., Zheng, H., Mei, T.: Look closer to see better: recurrent attention convolutional neural network for fine-grained image recognition. In: 2017 IEEE Conference on Computer Vision and Pattern Recognition (CVPR), pp. 4476–4484, July 2017
18. BelgiumTS Dataset. https://btsd.ethz.ch/shareddata/
19. Chinese Traffic Sign Database. http://www.nlpr.ia.ac.cn/pal/trafficdata/detection.html
20. The MASTIF datasets. http://www.zemris.fer.hr/~ssegvic/mastif/datasets.shtml
21. Russian Traffic sign recognition Dataset. http://graphics.cs.msu.ru/en/research/projects/imagerecognition/trafficsign

22. Spanish Traffic Sign Dataset. https://daus-lab.github.io/spanish-traffic-sign-dataset/
23. GTSRB Dataset. http://benchmark.ini.rub.de/?section=gtsrb&subsection=dataset
24. DITS - Data set of Italian Traffic Signs. http://users.diag.uniroma1.it/bloisi/ds/dits.html

MaskADNet: MOTS Based on ADNet

Anusha Aswath[✉] and Renu M. Rameshan[✉]

Indian Institute of Technology, Mandi, Himachal Pradesh, India
anusha.aswath@gmail.com, renumr@iitmandi.ac.in

Abstract. In this paper, we aim to perform multi-object tracking and segmentation (MOTS) of moving objects in traffic video datasets. A novel method for tracking multiple objects is proposed, which uses masked images as input for training ADNet [39], and we name it as MaskADNet. Segmentation mask prior for tracking using only foreground instances has shown significant improvements in tracking performance. Better online update using masked images and reduced tracking failures help achieve 10.57% and 12% increase in precision and success rates over the previous approach [2]. The segmentation masks obtained after tracking using MaskADNet have a better Jaccard index or Intersection over Union for masks. The network also achieves improvements in association of tracks with detection or re-identification of lost targets in multi-object tracking scenarios, with minimal changes in identity. The proposed method of tracking has shown that tracking using segmentation masks can achieve significant improvements for multi-object tracking and segmentation.

Keywords: MOTS · Masked input image · Multi-object tracking · Segmentation masks · Re-identification

1 Introduction

Advanced Driver Assistance Systems (ADAS) focus on camera, radar and lidar sensor fusion for classification, detection and tracking in traffic scenarios. Deep learning methods have revolutionized computer vision solutions and are used extensively in many computer vision products. But they suffer from the need of large annotated datasets for training. Data collection using test drives on interstate highways and city highways are done to record large videos. These recordings have around 1500000 frames each and require examination for labeling different objects like cars, trucks, pedestrians, lost cargo, traffic signs, among others. The labeling effort for one hour of recording is 149 h for cars and 79 h for pedestrians for fine pixel masks. Automation in labeling such large recordings is required to make the process of annotation efficient and to save time and effort.

In this paper, we aim to automate generation of ground truth segmentation masks for multiple objects in a video recording. This task requires simultaneous tracking and segmentation aided by detection. The accuracy that can be obtained by using simple bounding box tracking is limited [30]. The tracking performance can only be improved by using accurate segmentation. An MOTS (Multi-object

© Springer Nature Switzerland AG 2020
M. De Marsico et al. (Eds.): ICPRAM 2020, LNCS 12594, pp. 13–26, 2020.
https://doi.org/10.1007/978-3-030-66125-0_2

tracking and segmentation) based solution, where the segmentation improves the tracking performance is proposed in this paper. Our primary objective is to obtain accurate masks with minimal changes in identities for the purpose of annotation, which will be solved by MOTS technique. We propose to use an offline method involving a robust tracking algorithm that learns all initialized objects and solves for re-identification, along with producing the segmentation masks.

A single object tracker modified to track multiple objects in a video followed by segmentation of the tracked targets using polygon vertices was proposed in [2]. Though the method produced a good set of labeled masks, it has its own disadvantages. The generative method of predicting actions to locate the object in the next frame is learnt using bounding box information containing both the object and the background. The binary classifier also classifies different patches as object or background using every pixel information inside the bounding box. In case of appearance variations, occlusion or cluttered background the learning of actions or the binary classification easily drifts. This is because the set of actions do not reach the complete target leading to a bounding box that contains more of background than the object.

In this paper, we combine segmentation and tracking by learning a model that learns to track objects based on masked inputs. This method automatically suppresses temporally inconsistent tracks by using only the foreground information. The number of tracking failures are minimized by preventing model drift which improves online target update for changes in appearance, illumination, blur or fast motion during long term tracking of objects. The proposed method differs from that of MDT_RCM (Multi-Domain Tracking and Re-identification using Correlation Maps) [2] in the following aspects -

- A new model is trained for tracking using action sequences with masked images as input.
- It experiments with learning a binary classifier online using masked images that results in less number of tracking failures due to background changes.
- It also improves the association of re-detected patch with detections and re-identification of the target using a Siamese network for long-term tracking.

The main contributions in this paper are -

- The method proposed improves a single object-tracker to be used for multi-object tracking using segmentation masks.
- It solves the problem of mutli-object tracking and segmentation for generating accurate ground truth data using cues from appearance, motion and segmentation priors.

The rest of the paper is organized as follows: Sect. 2 gives the related work on tracking and segmentation methods, Sect. 3 gives details of the proposed method, followed by results on different datasets and conclusion in Sects. 4 and 5, respectively.

2   Related Work

Multi-target tracking (MOT) is the problem of simultaneously solving for the trajectories of individual objects, while maintaining their identities over time through occlusions, clutter and complex interactions. Multi-object tracking and segmentation (MOTS) extends multi-object tracking to utilize segmentation for tracking objects in video datasets. Video object segmentation (VOS) aims to segment foreground objects from background in a video. Video Instance Segmentation Tracking (VIS) [38] combines simultaneous segmentation and tracking for different single instance segmented objects in videos. Both MOTS and VIS addresses common challenges like occlusion, blur, fast motion, out-of-view and real-time processing. In the following subsections we discuss literature work related to MOT, VIS and MOTS.

2.1   Multi-object Tracking

Offline Methods. Tracking by detection is the most common approach where object detections are associated across frames. These methods either learn offline models based on a similarity measure to associate detections with tracklets. The offline method does not associate detection with history of the track in case of occlusions or re-identification. Generative models aim to model the appearance of the target offline. In [5], an appearance model was learned offline, which could not adapt to significant appearance changes. In order to solve this problem, some adaptive appearance models were proposed [14,26]. Pre-trained CNN models are used to obtain feature maps to correlate two images [27]. A fully convolutional Siamese network for correlation of a target and search patch was proposed [29] to learn similarity on targets between frames.

Online Methods. Tracking can also be performed using a discriminative approach, which define the tracking problem as a binary classification task between the foreground and background. It is important to update the target appearance model online to take into account appearance changes, cluttered background, blur or deformations. For discriminative models, the main issue has been improving the sample collection part to make the online trained classifier more robust [3,9,11,15]. Tracker based on online update based on bootstrapping from unlabeled samples collected in video sequence demonstrated good tracking results in videos [21]. Further, an update to the searching algorithm was performed using a set of actions and their histories for motion model [39]. A discriminative single object tracker can be used for tracking multiple objects [7] by solving the online update in MOT scenarios. The online update and re-identification problem was solved by using a Siamese tracker in [2].

2.2   Video Instance Segmentation

Video object Segmentation (VOS) depends on two methods - propagation-based methods and detection-based methods. The propagation methods use the temporally coherent information between frames by formulating it as object mask propagation using motion information [10, 22, 28, 35]. This works well for spatio-temporal smooth motion but fails during discontinuities in case of occlusion and fast motion. It also suffers from target drift once the target becomes unreliable. This is because a simple model adapted to first frame mask cannot generalize well to separate the foreground from background.

Detection-based methods [6, 18] model the target appearance and perform dense pixel classification of targets in a given frame. They work well on occluded objects, but since they are not temporally correlated they cannot accurately model the different appearance deformations of the target as the video sequence proceeds. An example of detection based video object segmentation method is Mask-RCNN [12]. For Video Instance Segmentation (VIS) [37], to assign an identity to each of the segmented masks, a new tracking branch was introduced as MaskTrack-RCNN. Siam-Mask [31] was proposed to track objects and create masks using a unified network for fast object tracking and segmentation. All new methods aim at using the unified approach for performing VIS.

2.3   Segmentation for Tracking

A fusion of appearance and motion models using deep learning was used to propagate segmentation in a fully-automated manner [13]. All of them try to link segmentation masks based on consistent object tracks.

On the other hand, work on using the segmentation masks to track in further frames is based on a Bayesian learning approach. A mask prior and appearance vector of the object with the background vector being the same for all frames was used in a Bayesian framework in [32]. Another deep learning based method fuses segmentation mask into its multi-channel features to perform tracking [17]. By using global information for multi-target tracking and local information for motion based segmentation, a joint multi-cut formulation for obtaining both was proposed in [16]. This method showed the importance of using point trajectories and local information for multi-object tracking.

Multi-object tracking and segmentation (MOTS) [30] solves for simultaneous detection, tracking and segmentation for tracking multiple objects using a single convolutional network called TrackR-CNN [30]. This method shows that MOTS can be achieved much more accurately by using a combined approach, as compared to using only bounding box tracks and single instance segmentation methods.

2.4   Semi-automatic Segmentation

Semi-automatic segmentation using cues from bounding box, scribbles, key points or edges by a human-in-the-loop provide interactive annotation for pixel masks. Inside a bounding box, DeepMask [24] can automatically produce dense pixel-wise prediction. Deep Extreme Cut [19] and Deep Grab Cut [36] offer a guided and interactive annotation method. All these methods do not offer easy corrections for pixel annotations. Hence, we propose to use polygon vertices for semantic instance segmentation generated through the deep learning based network in [1].

3   Multi-object Tracking and Segmentation Using MaskADNet

The proposed method (MaskADNet) tracks multiple targets by training ADNet [39] with inputs in the form of masked images. The network shows improved tracking results as compared to MDT_RCM [2], the baseline method. The number of resets during long-term tracking due to appearance variations in case of severe occlusion or out-of-view motion is reduced as compared to the baseline. It also shows significant improvement in precision and success rates for MOT scenarios with challenges like blur, illumination variation, fast motion or background clutter. This is due to improved tracking through action sequences and online update of the binary classifier using masked inputs.

3.1   Baseline Method

The network based on ADNet [39] was used to track objects using a set of actions based on the bounding box input. The sequence of actions taken were trained using reinforcement learning to reach a target in the frame from its previous position, till a stop action was reached or till a maximum of 20 sequential actions. The set of actions proceed based on the class score of the object being greater than a threshold. The action sequence is stopped when the class score is less than a threshold. Re-detection is performed by sampling patches around the lost track and selecting the patch with best class confidence score to continue tracking.

The network also adapted its weights in an online manner based on p-n (positive and negative) samples collected from past successfully tracked frames. The bounding box appearance information contain both foreground object and background. The tracker was extended to track multiple objects by using multiple branches (multi-domain learning) of the fully connected layers to capture individual motion information and online update.

Since the classifier score could not work for tracking failures or re-detection for MOT scenarios, for online update a dynamic threshold for each object based on the original target appearance was set. A Siamese network [4] for calculating the PSR (peak to side lobe ratio) value on the correlation maps was used for handling model drift. Using the dynamic threshold obtained by calculating the PSR value, the model was adapted online or a re-detection was accepted. The motion model helped in re-identification of inactive targets by assigning a search area. To perform segmentation another network that captures the object shape by predicting polygon vertices around the object to be segmented using PolyRNN++ [1] was integrated. The two networks for simultaneous tracking and segmentation were used in an annotation tool using a communication protocol between them [2].

3.2   MaskADNet

In this method, we improve the single object tracker ADNet using segmentation masks and thereby improve the MDT_RCM tracker by converting it into an

MOTS. The improvement in tracking thus achieved also improves the segmentation. Also, the segmentation masks aid in better tracking. The network performs better as compared to the baseline method in both single and multi-object tracking challenges that include occlusions, frequent disappearance or reappearance and during target interactions.

Network Architecture and Training. The network used for training is a VGG-M model and is trained in a manner similar to ADNet [39]. The inputs provided to the network are segmentation masks overlaid on images to obtained masked inputs as shown in Fig. 1. The network is trained for both supervised and reinforcement training through different video sequences for learning to take actions and tracking using class confidence scores.

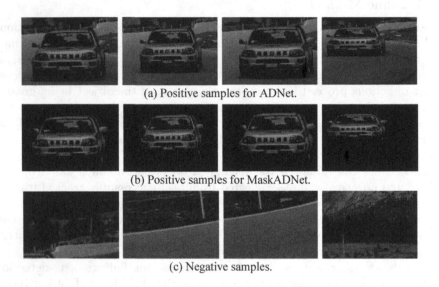

(a) Positive samples for ADNet.

(b) Positive samples for MaskADNet.

(c) Negative samples.

Fig. 1. Positive and negative samples used for supervised training.

Layers $fc6$ and $fc7$ are trained using supervised training through labels generated for action and class confidence layers. Sample patches are generated as positive and negative samples p_j using Gaussian and uniform noise added to the groundtruth box. The action label, obtained by using only the positive samples containing only foreground information, is the action leading to maximum IoU with ground truth box G. The class label is a binary label of 1 if there is an IoU of more than 0.7 and 0 otherwise.

$$l_j^{act} = \arg\max_a \text{IoU}(p_j^a, G)$$

$$l_j^{cls} = \begin{cases} 1, & \text{if IoU}(p_j, G) > 0.7 \\ 0, & \text{otherwise} \end{cases} \qquad (1)$$

The network is trained with cross-entropy loss between the action labels l_j^{act} and the predicted action and the class labels l_j^{cls} and the predicted class by the network. As the network is trained by using only the foreground information, its learning for predicting action sequences based on class scores is different from that of ADNet. Examples of positive and negative samples for MaskADNet are shown in Fig. 1.

For reinforcement learning, the network is trained through rewards obtained during the tracking simulation. Tracking from frame l to frame $l+1$ using the motion model (through action vector of past 10 actions concatenated to layer $fc5$) is used to obtain the sequence of actions. On frame $l+1$ the reward is the intersection over union (IoU) of the tracked box with the ground truth. The cost function for re-reinforcement learning is changed to include the IoU of mask to learn better in case of occlusions or out-of-view motion. The reward function is now modified as -

$$r = \begin{cases} 1, & \text{if IoU (box and mask)}(tracked_l, ground\_truth_{l+1}) > 0.7 \\ -1, & \text{otherwise} \end{cases} \qquad (2)$$

During inference, for tracking multiple objects we use the multi-domain network [2] for the last layers for tracking multiple objects as shown in Fig. 2. The online update for action and class layers is through masked images for multiple objects obtained using tracked boxes and segmentation network.

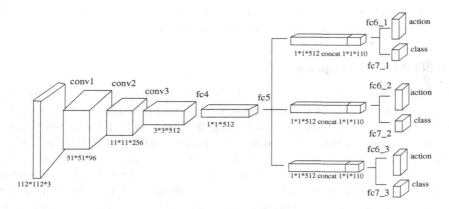

Fig. 2. Multi-object tracking network by using layers conv1, conv2, conv3, fc4 and fc5 from trained model of MaskADNet.

Dataset for Training. For training the network on segmentation masks, we use DAVIS 2016 dataset [23] for video object segmentation and DAVIS 2017 dataset [25] for video instance segmentation. The dataset is divided into 70 train sequences, 30 validation sequences and 40 test sequences. Training is performed for supervised learning using generated patches and their action and class labels for 30 epochs. The network is then trained for reinforcement learning for 30

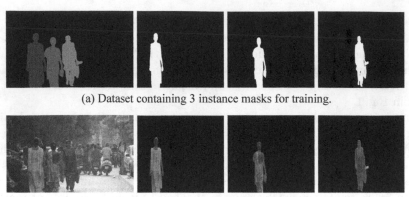

(a) Dataset containing 3 instance masks for training.

(b) Original and masked image inputs.

Fig. 3. Network trained on instance segmentation masks from DAVIS 2017 dataset.

epochs to track using the motion model of past 10 action vectors. An example sequence from DAVIS 2017 dataset is shown in Fig. 3.

4   Results and Discussion

A brief description of the datasets used for training and evaluation is provided in the first section. This is followed by discussion on the results obtained based on the various metrics for tracking and segmentation.

4.1   Dataset Description

The DAVIS 2016 dataset consists 50 high quality videos with 3455 annotated frames, all captured at 24 fps covering scenarios like occlusions, motion blur and appearance changes for different single targets. The DAVIS 2017 dataset consist of 150 sequences, totaling 10459 annotated frames and 376 objects. The DAVIS 2017 dataset have more than one annotated object in the scene and with more complexity in terms of distractors, fine structures, occlusions and faster motion.

We also perform evaluation on the OTB-100 dataset [34] for comparison with the baseline approach. For long term multi-object tracking the network is evaluated on MOT-16 dataset [20] and compared with the previous approach. OTB-100 dataset consists of 100 video sequences covering different challenges like illumination and scale variations, fast motion, motion blur, occlusions, deformations etc. MOT16 dataset has severe occlusions, interacting targets and frequent disappearance and appearance of objects.

Metrics Used for Evaluation. For evaluation of the proposed tracker under different scenarios like occlusion, blur, fast motion or illumination changes, precision and success values are plotted [33].

1. **Precision Plot**- This plot calculates the number percentage of frames within the threshold for the center location error, which is defined as the average Euclidean distance between the center locations of the tracked targets and the manually labeled ground truths.
2. **Success Plot**- Another evaluation metric is the bounding box overlap. To measure the performance on a sequence of frames, we count the number of successful frames whose overlap is larger than the given threshold.

The evaluation is also be performed on test sequences of DAVIS 2016 and DAVIS 2017 dataset for comparing the two networks (MDT_RCM and MaskADNet) for segmentation output.

1. **Jaccard Index**- It gives the overlap or intersection over union of the tracked mask and the ground truth mask.
2. **Area of False Negatives**- This gives the number of pixels that are not marked as masks but are actually having pixels with mask. This measure is used to find the accuracy of the tracker to cover the entire object.
3. **Number of Tracking Failures**- This gives the number of times the sequence of actions failed to track it in the next frames. The tracking failure occurs when the class confidence score of the tracked patch is less than the threshold for class score. This measure shows how well MaskADNet is trained using masked inputs to track using actions as compared to the baseline method.

4.2 Evaluation

Figure 4 shows the comparison graphs for precision and success plots on OTB-100 dataset with respect to the ADNet, the MDT_RCM [2] (Multi-Domain Tracker with Re-identification using Correlation Maps), Re3 [8] and MaskADNet. We see that the precision at location error threshold of 20 pixels are 74.2, 40.5, 80.7 and 91.27 for ADNet, Re3, the MDT_RCM tracker and MaskADNet respectively. The success at an overlap ratio of 0.5 are 78.6, 30.8, 80.6 and 92.6 respectively. The results for methods other than MaskADNet are taken from [2].

The comparison on DAVIS dataset for Jaccard index, area of false negatives and number of tracking failures is shown in Table 1. The results are compared for MDT_RCM and MaskADNet on the short video sequences from test data sets. The samples for online update for both the networks are different - first has bounding box samples containing both foreground and background pixels and the latter has only the masked image as positive samples.

The results in Table 1 show that the model trained using masks is able to track the object more efficiently. This is shown by lesser area of false negatives indicating better masks within the tracked boxes. It also has lesser tracking failures using the action sequence to track objects and hence requires lesser re-detections. An example sequence -parkour from DAVIS 17 dataset having a single tracking failure as compared to 32 lost tracks is shown in Fig. 5.

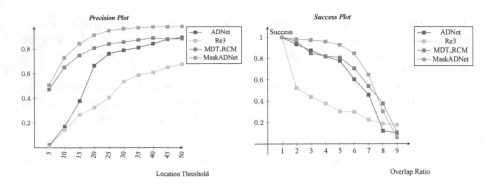

Fig. 4. Precision and Success Plots for 100 OTB data sequences (single object tracking).

For evaluating the proposed method for long-term tracking we use the MOT16 train sequences. The precision and success plots on MOT16-02 video are shown in Fig. 6. The results for methods other than MaskADNet are taken from [2] for MOT16-02 dataset. Since ADNet is a single object tracker, it is run on each instance to be tracked separately and the plot is obtained by averaging over all the objects.

The results show best performance in comparison with [2] as there are less tracking failures leading to 1) less learning of re-detected patches 2) better model for motion through action history vector. Since the drift has reduced the corresponding tracking time has also come down, though we have not measured the exact time measurements. The Siamese network, in case of tracking failure, is used to better associate the re-detected patch with detection in the search area around the object.

Table 1. Results of MaskADNet and MDT_RCM on DAVIS 2017 test sequences.

VideoSet	Jaccard index	False negatives	No. of tracking failures	Jaccard index	False negatives	No. of tracking failures
	MaskADNet			MDT_RCM		
car-roundabout	**0.98**	**848.27**	0	0.78	10025.88	0
drift-chicane	**0.66**	**3323.62**	2	0.64	3502.55	9
goat	**0.94**	**1606.32**	0	0.90	2623.14	1
paragliding-launch	**0.91**	**944.06**	1	0.64	2831.76	4
parkour	**0.92**	**1685.66**	1	0.84	2853.86	32
scooter-black	**0.98**	**153.61**	0	0.84	1275.28	9
scooter-board	**0.77**	**3304.61**	7	0.63	7888.44	51
Sheep	**0.86**	**371.52**	0	0.55	1207.42	5

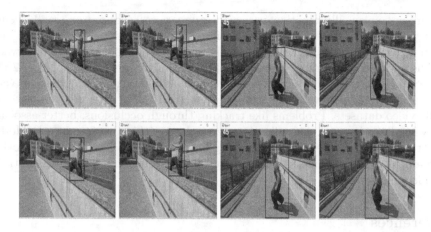

Fig. 5. First row show tracking failures from frame 20 to 21 and frame 45 to 46 for MDT_RCM framework. Second row shows no tracking failure by using MaskADNet.

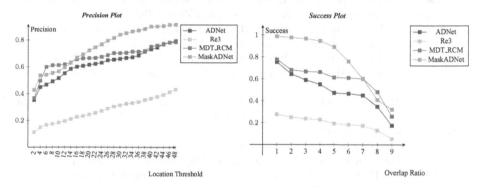

Fig. 6. Precision and Success Plots for MOT16-02 sequence (multi-object tracking).

5   Conclusion

In this paper, we solve the problem of multi-object tracking and segmentation (MOTS) using MaskADNet. Tracking is performed using segmentation masks as inputs instead of bounding boxes. By using this approach, we were able to obtain significant improvements for single and multi-object tracking scenarios. The new model also led to an improved motion-based tracking, as there are less number of failures in taking actions. This resulted in better re-identifications by re-detection over the search area which is determined by the motion model. The improvements for single object tracking were 10.57% and 12% for precision and success respectively. We obtain approximately 90% reduction in tracking failures using action sequences with MaskADNet to track a target in the next frame. This reduces the need for using re-detections for classifier update or associating with detections in frames. It performs best in short sequences with challenges like background noise, illumination variation, appearance changes or small occlusions. In long-term tracking for association of tracked patches with detections and re-identification of inactive targets, significant improvements were observed.

The entire framework of using an improved multi-object tracker (MaskAD-Net), Siamese network for data association and segmentation using polygon vertices for annotation solved for automatic segmentation of different instances in traffic video datasets. Problems like tracking through occlusions, better association with detection or re-identification were solved within this framework. Modifying the baseline tracker by training using segmentation masks showed improved multi-object tracking and segmentation results for obtaining mask labels in traffic video datasets.

References

1. Acuna, D., Ling, H., Kar, A., Fidler, S.: Efficient interactive annotation of segmentation datasets with polygon-RNN++. In: Proceedings of the IEEE Conference on Computer Vision and Pattern Recognition, pp. 859–868 (2018)
2. Aswath, A., Rameshan, R., Krishnan, B., Ponkumar, S.: Segmentation of moving objects in traffic video datasets. In: Marsico, M.D., di Baja, G.S., Fred, A.L.N. (eds.) Proceedings of the 9th International Conference on Pattern Recognition Applications and Methods, ICPRAM 2020, Valletta, Malta, 22–24 February 2020, pp. 321–332. SCITEPRESS (2020)
3. Babenko, B., Yang, M.H., Belongie, S.: Visual tracking with online multiple instance learning. In: 2009 IEEE Conference on Computer Vision and Pattern Recognition, pp. 983–990. IEEE (2009)
4. Bertinetto, L., Valmadre, J., Henriques, J.F., Vedaldi, A., Torr, P.H.S.: Fully-convolutional siamese networks for object tracking. In: Hua, G., Jégou, H. (eds.) ECCV 2016, Part II. LNCS, vol. 9914, pp. 850–865. Springer, Cham (2016). https://doi.org/10.1007/978-3-319-48881-3_56
5. Black, M.J., Jepson, A.D.: Eigentracking: robust matching and tracking of articulated objects using a view-based representation. Int. J. Comput. Vis. **26**(1), 63–84 (1998)
6. Caelles, S., Maninis, K.K., Pont-Tuset, J., Leal-Taixé, L., Cremers, D., Van Gool, L.: One-shot video object segmentation. In: Proceedings of the IEEE Conference on Computer Vision and Pattern Recognition, pp. 221–230 (2017)
7. Chu, Q., Ouyang, W., Li, H., Wang, X., Liu, B., Yu, N.: Online multi-object tracking using CNN-based single object tracker with spatial-temporal attention mechanism. In: Proceedings of the IEEE International Conference on Computer Vision, pp. 4836–4845 (2017)
8. Gordon, D., Farhadi, A., Fox, D.: Re3: real-time recurrent regression networks for visual tracking of generic objects. IEEE Robot. Autom. Lett. **3**(2), 788–795 (2018)
9. Grabner, H., Grabner, M., Bischof, H.: Real-time tracking via on-line boosting. In: BMVC, vol. 1, p. 6 (2006)
10. Grundmann, M., Kwatra, V., Han, M., Essa, I.: Efficient hierarchical graph-based video segmentation. In: 2010 IEEE Computer Society Conference on Computer Vision and Pattern Recognition, pp. 2141–2148. IEEE (2010)
11. Hare, S., et al.: Struck: structured output tracking with kernels. IEEE Trans. Pattern Anal. Mach. Intell. **38**(10), 2096–2109 (2015)

12. Hu, Y.T., Huang, J.B., Schwing, A.: MaskRNN: instance level video object segmentation. In: Advances in Neural Information Processing Systems, pp. 325–334 (2017)
13. Jain, S.D., Xiong, B., Grauman, K.: FusionSeg: learning to combine motion and appearance for fully automatic segmentation of generic objects in videos. In: 2017 IEEE Conference on Computer Vision and Pattern Recognition (CVPR), pp. 2117–2126. IEEE (2017)
14. Jepson, A.D., Fleet, D.J., El-Maraghi, T.F.: Robust online appearance models for visual tracking. IEEE Trans. Pattern Anal. Mach. Intell. **25**(10), 1296–1311 (2003)
15. Kalal, Z., Matas, J., Mikolajczyk, K.: P-N learning: bootstrapping binary classifiers by structural constraints. In: 2010 IEEE Computer Society Conference on Computer Vision and Pattern Recognition, pp. 49–56. IEEE (2010)
16. Keuper, M., Tang, S., Zhongjie, Y., Andres, B., Brox, T., Schiele, B.: A multi-cut formulation for joint segmentation and tracking of multiple objects. arXiv preprint arXiv:1607.06317 (2016)
17. Lee, S.H., Jang, W.D., Kim, C.S.: Tracking-by-segmentation using superpixel-wise neural network. IEEE Access **6**, 54982–54993 (2018)
18. Maninis, K.K., et al.: Video object segmentation without temporal information. IEEE Trans. Pattern Anal. Mach. Intell. **41**(6), 1515–1530 (2018)
19. Maninis, K.K., Caelles, S., Pont-Tuset, J., Van Gool, L.: Deep extreme cut: from extreme points to object segmentation. In: Proceedings of the IEEE Conference on Computer Vision and Pattern Recognition, pp. 616–625 (2018)
20. Milan, A., Leal-Taixé, L., Reid, I., Roth, S., Schindler, K.: MOT16: A benchmark for multi-object tracking. arXiv preprint arXiv:1603.00831 (2016)
21. Nam, H., Han, B.: Learning multi-domain convolutional neural networks for visual tracking. In: Proceedings of the IEEE Conference on Computer Vision and Pattern Recognition, pp. 4293–4302 (2016)
22. Perazzi, F., Khoreva, A., Benenson, R., Schiele, B., Sorkine-Hornung, A.: Learning video object segmentation from static images. In: Proceedings of the IEEE Conference on Computer Vision and Pattern Recognition, pp. 2663–2672 (2017)
23. Perazzi, F., Pont-Tuset, J., McWilliams, B., Van Gool, L., Gross, M., Sorkine-Hornung, A.: A benchmark dataset and evaluation methodology for video object segmentation. In: Proceedings of the IEEE Conference on Computer Vision and Pattern Recognition, pp. 724–732 (2016)
24. Pinheiro, P.O., Lin, T.-Y., Collobert, R., Dollár, P.: Learning to refine object segments. In: Leibe, B., Matas, J., Sebe, N., Welling, M. (eds.) ECCV 2016, Part I. LNCS, vol. 9905, pp. 75–91. Springer, Cham (2016). https://doi.org/10.1007/978-3-319-46448-0_5
25. Pont-Tuset, J., Perazzi, F., Caelles, S., Arbeláez, P., Sorkine-Hornung, A., Van Gool, L.: The 2017 davis challenge on video object segmentation. arXiv preprint arXiv:1704.00675 (2017)
26. Ross, D., Lim, J., Lin, R., Yang, M.: Incremental learning for robust visual tracking. Int. J. Comput. Vis. **25**(8), 1034–1040 (2008). https://doi.org/10.1007/s11263-007-0075-7
27. Tao, R., Gavves, E., Smeulders, A.W.: Siamese instance search for tracking. In: Proceedings of the IEEE Conference on Computer Vision and Pattern Recognition, pp. 1420–1429 (2016)
28. Tsai, D., Flagg, M., Nakazawa, A., Rehg, J.M.: Motion coherent tracking using multi-label MRF optimization. Int. J. Comput. Vis. **100**(2), 190–202 (2012)

29. Valmadre, J., Bertinetto, L., Henriques, J., Vedaldi, A., Torr, P.H.: End-to-end representation learning for correlation filter based tracking. In: Proceedings of the IEEE Conference on Computer Vision and Pattern Recognition, pp. 2805–2813 (2017)
30. Voigtlaender, P., et al.: MOTS: multi-object tracking and segmentation. In: Proceedings of the IEEE Conference on Computer Vision and Pattern Recognition, pp. 7942–7951 (2019)
31. Wang, Q., Zhang, L., Bertinetto, L., Hu, W., Torr, P.H.: Fast online object tracking and segmentation: a unifying approach. In: Proceedings of the IEEE Conference on Computer Vision and Pattern Recognition, pp. 1328–1338 (2019)
32. Winn, J., Blake, A.: Generative affine localisation and tracking. In: Advances in Neural Information Processing Systems, pp. 1505–1512 (2005)
33. Wu, Y., Lim, J., Yang, M.H.: Online object tracking: a benchmark. In: Proceedings of the IEEE Conference on Computer Vision and Pattern Recognition, pp. 2411–2418 (2013)
34. Wu, Y., Lim, J., Yang, M.H.: Object tracking benchmark. IEEE Trans. Pattern Anal. Mach. Intell. $37(9)$, 1834–1848 (2015)
35. Wug Oh, S., Lee, J.Y., Sunkavalli, K., Joo Kim, S.: Fast video object segmentation by reference-guided mask propagation. In: Proceedings of the IEEE Conference on Computer Vision and Pattern Recognition, pp. 7376–7385 (2018)
36. Xu, N., Price, B., Cohen, S., Yang, J., Huang, T.S.: Deep interactive object selection. In: Proceedings of the IEEE Conference on Computer Vision and Pattern Recognition, pp. 373–381 (2016)
37. Yang, L., Fan, Y., Xu, N.: Video instance segmentation. In: Proceedings of the IEEE International Conference on Computer Vision, pp. 5188–5197 (2019)
38. Yao, R., Lin, G., Xia, S., Zhao, J., Zhou, Y.: Video object segmentation and tracking: A survey. arXiv preprint arXiv:1904.09172 (2019)
39. Yun, S., Choi, J., Yoo, Y., Yun, K., Young Choi, J.: Action-decision networks for visual tracking with deep reinforcement learning. In: Proceedings of the IEEE Conference on Computer Vision and Pattern Recognition, pp. 2711–2720 (2017)

Dimensionality Reduction and Attention Mechanisms for Extracting Affective State from Sound Spectrograms

George Pikramenos[1,2]([⊠]), Konstantinos Kechagias[1], Theodoros Psallidas[2], Georgios Smyrnis[3], Evaggelos Spyrou[2], and Stavros Perantonis[2]

[1] Department of Informatics and Telecommunications,
National Kapodistrian University of Athens, Athens, Greece
{gpik,kkech}@di.uoa.gr
[2] National Center for Scientific Research, Demokritos, Athens, Greece
{espyrou,sper}@iit.demokritos.gr
[3] School of Electrical and Computer Engineering,
National Technical University of Athens, Athens, Greece
el14007@central.ntua.gr

Abstract. Emotion recognition (ER) has drawn the interest of many researchers in the field of human-computer interaction, being central in such applications as assisted living and personalized content suggestion. When considering the implementation of ER capable systems, if they are to be widely adopted in daily life, one must take into account that methods for emotion recognition should work on data collected in an unobtrusive way. Out of the possible data modalities for affective state analysis, which include video and biometrics, speech is considered the least intrusive and for this reason has drawn the focus of many research efforts. In this chapter, we discuss methods for analyzing the non-linguistic component of vocalized speech for the purposes of ER. In particular, we propose a method for producing lower dimensional representations of sound spectrograms which respect their temporal structure. Moreover, we explore possible methods for analyzing such representations, including shallow methods, recurrent neural networks and attention mechanisms. Our models are evaluated on data taken from popular, public datasets for emotion analysis with promising results.

Keywords: Sentiment analysis · Speech analysis · Bag-of-visual-words

1 Introduction

Automatic human emotional state recognition constitutes a recent trend in the broader research area of human computer interaction [1] and has several potential applications in everyday life. Several data modalities are typically used for the purposes of ER. Usually, information is obtained through sensors, placed on the subject's body or environment. For example, bio-metric sensors, cameras

M. De Marsico et al. (Eds.): ICPRAM 2020, LNCS 12594, pp. 27–45, 2020.
https://doi.org/10.1007/978-3-030-66125-0_3

or microphones may be utilized. Despite that video data has become the main public means of self-expression [2], cameras are considered to be more invasive than microphones [3]. Body sensors constitute a reasonable practical alternative but they may cause discomfort, especially when used continuously for a long time. Thus, due to the reasons highlighted above, many researchers prefer microphones for many emotion recognition applications. As such, it is typical for research works in sentiment analysis to focus on sound data.

In particular, in this work we assume data is collected by microphones capturing the subject's vocalized speech. Although alternatives exist, for example analyzing non-verbal vocal expressions (*see* e.g. [4]), the adopted approach is very common in ER literature. Vocalized speech is comprised of a *linguistic* and a *non-linguistic* component. The former is made up of the speaker's pronounced vocal patterns, while the latter captures the speakers' pronunciation of these patterns. That is, the linguistic and the non-linguistic part of speech are respectively *what/how* the subject said/(it) [5]. Respectively, we say a method is linguistic/non-linguistic if it analyzes the linguistic/non-linguistic content of speech.

A key benefit of non-linguistic methods is that they create models that are intrinsically language-independent. Linguistic methods couple the emotion recognition problem with speech recognition. For this reason, the language present in the training data limits the generalization capabilities of the produced model. On the other hand, non-linguistic methods do not require an intermediate speech recognition step and, instead, only rely on pronunciation. This does not make the problem simple, since cultural particularities majorly affect the non-linguistic content of speech. This is true even when handling data containing a single language, since there are many different sentences, speakers, speaking styles and rates [6]. Thus, in this chapter we focus on non-linguistic methods.

As is often the case in many machine learning tasks, an important step in non-linguistic methods is the extraction of an appropriate representation of the speech signal. Earlier methods for sentiment analysis were mainly based on hand-crafted features such as the rhythm and pitch intensity of the signal [7]. Latter methods made popular the use of transformations on the retrieved signal to produce spectro-temporal features capturing important short and long term characteristics regarding the emotional content of speech. Typical in the literature is the use of Fourier and wavelet transforms [8]. In particular, many works utilize short-time Fourier transforms to generate spectrograms of the speech signal in order to perform emotion recognition [10–12].

An issue that often arises when working with spectrograms in emotion recognition is the dimensionality of the data. For this reason, we investigate schemes for producing concise representations of spectrograms which preserve important data aspects such as the temporal structure. In particular, in line with previous work [13], we propose the use of a visual word vocabulary extracted from the data as a dimensionality reduction technique. We further extend the work in [13] by considering the analysis of the extracted representations using neural networks with attention mechanisms as an alternative to the previously proposed recurrent network modelling.

2   Related Literature Review

As discussed in the previous section, sentiment recognition that incorporates emotional signals from vocalized speech is the subject of many research efforts. Earlier approaches to both linguistic and non-linguistic methods utilized shallow machine learning methods over hand-crafted features to extract affective content. In [15], the authors utilize low level audio features, such as prosodic features, MFCCs and formant frequencies, in conjunction with visual features extracted from the speaker. They demonstrate a substantial improvement in accuracy when both modalities are used. Similarly, but focusing only on audio signals, the authors in [16] utilize Hidden Markov Models to analyze the emotional content of data represented in low level audio features. Their results highlight the value of analyzing the sequential structure of the signal and the value of using audio features.

The use of computer vision techniques on spectrograms extracted from speech signals has emerged as a common practice in sentiment analysis recently. In [17], the authors utilize keypoint descriptors to produce visual features of spectrograms. These descriptors are then clustered to produce a visual vocabulary, which is in turn used to construct a Bag-of-Visual-Words (BoVW) representation. However, this representation can prove to be rigid, with each keypoint assigned to a single visual word, even if closely matching more than one. Moreover, no information about the temporal relations encoded in the spectrogram are encoded in the representation. An alternative, representation using sequences of *soft* histograms is explored in this chapter following the work in [13].

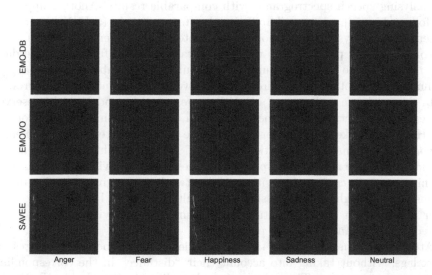

Fig. 1. (Figure taken from [13]) Spectrograms produced by applying DTSTFT with window size 40 ms and step size 20 ms to randomly selected audio samples from each of the considered emotions and datasets. The used audio clips have length 2 s and where appropriately cropped when necessary. The vertical axis corresponds to frequency while the horizontal axis corresponds to time (Figure best viewed in color).

Researchers have also studied emotion extraction from text data, which can be seen as a form or representation of speech or an intermediate step for linguistic methods. In particular, [34], analyze text derived from online sources to identify positive and negative emotional content. This is accomplished using syntactic and semantic preprocessing of text, and utilizing an SVM classifier. Such lexical features can also be used for analyzing vocalized speech, as shown in [19], where an ASR system is suggested to produce text from speech, and then, both audio and text features are used to analyze emotion. A similar fusion of audio and text, is suggested in [35], but there the text is available and does not need to be extracted.

More recent approaches for sentiment analysis make use of deep learning methods to extract representations automatically. In particular, the use of computer vision techniques based on neural networks for emotion recognition has spread significantly. In [24], the authors analyze spectrogram representations, using convolutional layers to extract representations which preserves the structure of the image. The features produced by this analysis are fed to a classifier, leading to good performing models. Other works have proposed similar methods based on CNNs [10–12].

The value of the temporal structure in speech data for the purposes of recognising affective state is highlighted by several works which utilize recurrent neural network classifiers to obtain regularized models. In [53], a bidirectional LSTM is used on both audio and visual features extracted from the facial image and speech of the speaker, demonstrating the capacity of these models for the task. In [14], the authors propose the use of both LSTMs and CNNs in conjunction, for analysing speech spectrograms, with comparable results. Another approach was followed in [54], where probabilistic echo state networks (π-ESNs) were used for sentiment analysis. The authors further note that recurrent versions of these networks not only perform very well on the task, but can further handle data with no labels, due to their unsupervised nature which enables them to adjust the number of emotions as required. π-ESNs were fed with acoustic features.

In this work, we make use of a BoVW representation model which preserves the temporal structure in the spectrogram, in a similar fashion to the work in [13]. However, unlike previous work, we propose the use of attention-based neural networks for the analysis of emotional content. It is shown through experiments that for reasonable numbers of words, the representation relying on sequences of soft histograms in conjunction with neural networks leveraging attention mechanisms leads to high quality classification results. Below we briefly review some other works which utilize attention mechanisms for supervised learning tasks related to speech and emotional processing.

Attention mechanisms allow modeling of dependencies between features, or index lags, without taking into account their "distance" in the corresponding input/output sequences. These mechanisms have been widely used in NLP tasks [21–23], as well as in speech recognition, particularly with self attention [29]. In [28], a new network architecture was proposed, which combines deep convolutional neural networks and attention mechanisms for analyzing images. This builds on the work in [30], which converts the self-attention mechanism to work with a 2D matrix instead of a vector. A similar approach can be found in [31]. In our experimental section, the *residual attention network* proposed in [28], is utilized with the entire spectrogram as input, as a benchmark for our methods.

Recently, neural networks leveraging attention mechanisms have also been proposed for recognizing sentiment. In [58], image processing attention based neural networks are utilized for tracking the affective state of the subject. In [59], the authors proposed an attention based model for the extraction of emotion from images with multiple subjects, while in [60], networks with self-attention are implemented for speech emotion recognition with very good results. However, unlike our work, in [60] the authors provide fixed length fragments of the sound waveform in time domain representation to the classifier. As argued in [60] self-attention captures long-term dependencies in the input signal which are essential to effective emotion recognition. The same intuition drives our approach but instead of processing the raw sound waveform, we analyze the sequence of spectral contents produced by the sliding window in the discrete-time short-time fourier transform. We found that self-attention is more effective than the LSTM approach proposed in our previous work [13].

3   Methodology

In this section we give an end-to-end detailed description of our emotion recognition pipeline. This includes the representation extraction from the raw sound waveform and the process of training the classifier.

3.1   BoVW Representation Building

The first step for building our vocalized speech representation, is a subsampling procedure on the original sound signal (in time domain), which yields a set of measurements $\{s(t_k)\}_{k=0}^{N-1}$. In turn, we perform the Discrete-Time Short-Time Fourier Transform [7], to obtain a two-dimensional spectrogram. This is essentially a 2-dimensional array described by the mathematical formula,

$$S(k, n) = \sum_{k=0}^{N-1} s(t_k) w(t_k - nT_s) e^{-\frac{2k\pi it_k}{N_w}}, \tag{1}$$

where N_w is the number of samples in each window and

$$w(t - \tau) = \begin{cases} 1, & |t - \tau| \leq T_w \\ 0, & o/w \end{cases} \tag{2}$$

is a kernel function modelling a sliding window which helps us extract short-term features from the signal. The parameters of the sliding window may be tuned according to the specific problem at hand. Other choices of w are also possible [7]. A step size T_s is used when sliding the window over the entire range of the signal.

The result is converted into a grayscale image I. In Fig. 1, we give visualizations from random samples for each of five classes of emotions, from three widely used datasets for sentiment analysis. Both in Fig. 1 and in our performed experiments (*see* Sect. 4), each audio clip was cropped to be of duration 2 s, the window size was 40 ms and the step size 20 ms.

After obtaining the speech spectrograms, we next define a grid of keypoints, each specified by a pair of pixel coordinates and a scale parameter. For each, a keypoint descriptor is obtained using ORB [20], with 128 features, following the work in [13]. Previous work [17] has also considered the use of SIFT/SURF descriptors. The obtained descriptors are latter used to create a visual vocabulary of words, which is in turn used to generate lower dimensional histogram representations of the spectrogram.

Having obtained the ORB descriptors for each image, a clustering algorithm is executed over the entire set of descriptors, for each image and each keypoint in the dataset, and a visual word pool $\mathcal{P} = \{w_i\}_i$ is generated. The size of $\mathcal{P}$, corresponds to the amount of clusters generated by the clustering algorithm. For example, using a standard k-means clustering algorithm we can control the size of the vocabulary through our choice of k. In [17], given a pool of words, a histogram is generated to represent an image by assigning each descriptor to its closest word and counting the times each word gets assigned a point. In [13], a *soft* histogram is used instead. Given a descriptor x, the l_2-distance from each word w_i is computed, denoted $d_i(x)$, and a vector h^x is obtained by computing the softmax over the distances to all words. In more detail, the ith coordinate is expressed by,

$$h_i^x = \frac{e^{-d_i(x)}}{\sum_{j \in \mathcal{P}} e^{-d_j(x)}}. \tag{3}$$

Then, image I is represented as a soft histogram as,

$$h(I) = \sum_{x \in I} h^x. \tag{4}$$

Note that h_i^x can be seen as a soft candidacy score of x to each word i, as opposed to the hard candidacy score used in [17]. Note also that if a single word w_i is much closer to a keypoint x than all other words, then $h_i^x \approx 1$ and $h_j^x \approx 0$ for each $j \neq i$. For such keypoints, the extracted soft and hard histogram representations are similar. However, keypoints that have comparable distances to many words are better described by their soft candidacy scores.

The representation extraction methodology is also provided in pseudocode in Procedure 1.

Remark 1. If a sufficiently large vocabulary is used, hard histograms may describe spectrograms sufficiently well. However, an increased number of visual words increases both inference and preprocessing complexity and also the dimensionality of the representation. The benefit of soft histograms is that they allow to better describe the spectrogram while using fewer words.

Remark 2. Alternatively, the soft-histogram procedure above can be seen as executing a form of fuzzy clustering to generate a fuzzy visual vocabulary. In fact a similar result could be achieved by running some fuzzy clustering algorithm, e.g., gaussian mixture clustering [57], and directly computing the sum of the soft candidacy scores of each keypoint in a given image to obtain the soft histogram representation. Obviously, another soft candidacy score function could be utilized to yield alternative representations.

3.2   Choosing Target Variables

At this point we must discuss some details regarding the sentiment extraction task. Emotion recognition is usually treated as a supervised learning task, and thus the existence of labeled training data is assumed. In this subsection we briefly discuss the possible ways to label data for sentiment analysis, as these emerge from the most popular datasets in the community. Both categorical and continuous labels are widely used in the literature, each with pros and cons. Most existing datasets which utilize categorical labels (*see* for example, [25–27]) are based in Plutchik's theory [47] of emotions, which argues that there are eight basic emotions and all other emotions are derived by combinations of these. The eight basic emotions are joy, trust, expectation, fear, sadness, disgust, anger, and surprise.

Procedure 1. Pseudocode for soft-histogram extraction (Taken from [13]).

Input: Data of subsampled audio signals D, parameter set λ;
Result: Soft histogram representation of elements in D;
\# Compute Spectrograms
$\hat{D}, \hat{S} \leftarrow \{\}, \{\}$;
for *each signal S in D* **do**
$\quad$ $\hat{s} \leftarrow DTSTFT(s, \lambda(T_s, T_w))$;
$\quad$ keypoints $\leftarrow$ get_grid($\hat{s}, \lambda$(resolution)) ;
$\quad$ descriptors $\leftarrow$ ORB(keypoints);
$\quad$ $\hat{S} \leftarrow \hat{S} \cup \{\hat{s}\}$;
$\quad$ $\hat{D} \leftarrow \hat{D} \cup \{\text{descriptors}\}$;
end
\# Compute Visual Vocabulary
words $\leftarrow$ Clustering($\hat{D}, \lambda$(vocabulary_size));
\# Compute Soft Histograms
$H \leftarrow \{\}$;
for *each set of descriptors* **d** *in $\hat{D}$* **do**
$\quad$ histo $\leftarrow$ **0**;
$\quad$ **for** *each descriptor d in* **d** **do**
$\quad\quad$ histo $\leftarrow$ histo $+$ soft_score(d, *words*);
$\quad$ **end**
$\quad$ $H \leftarrow H \cup \{histo\}$;
end

Typically, a subset of these emotions is used as a label set together with an additional "neutral" class, which indicates the absence of an emotional signal.

The benefit of the categorical labels approach is that it leads to models which are easier to interpret and validate than those produced by continuous labels approaches. On the other hand, the separation between these emotions may not be clear in certain situations and in addition, many affective states may not be well captured by this discretization. For this reason some researchers choose real-valued target variables to capture sentiment [46]. This approach typically relies on the PAD model [32], which breaks down emotion into three components, namely, Pleasure-Arousal-Dominance, each represented by a real number. Arguably, this approach is more effective in capturing emotional diversity. However, model interpretation and validation becomes much harder under continuous labels. In this work we follow the discrete target variable approach and treat ER as a classification task because it is more intuitive for the reader. However, the described methods can easily be adopted to work on real-valued labels.

3.3   Temporal Structure Preserving Representation

An important limitation of the BoVW model, as described so far, is that it does not take into account the temporal structure of matched visual words present in the spectrogram. In this section we propose a modification on the plain BoVW model to capture this temporal structure. Recall that the columns in the produced spectrograms correspond to different positions of a sliding window. This can be taken into account when designing our model to make it more robust. In particular, following the approach in [13], spectrograms are represented as a sequence of soft histograms, over visual words appearing in each column of the spectrogram. In particular, after each descriptor in the spectrogram is matched to a visual word, every column of descriptors (corresponding to all scales) is used to produce a soft histogram. Then, this sequence of soft-histograms is used to represent the spectrogram (Fig. 2).

Note that this sequential representation of spectrograms, has the capacity to encode the input's temporal structure. In particular, note that the histogram representation, is insensitive to shuffling the columns of the spectrogram. Randomly shuffling the columns of a spectrogram, produces a spectrogram which corresponds to a very different audio signal than the one that we are interested in analyzing. However, both of these signals will have the same BoVW representation. On the other hand, the sequential representation considered here is sensitive to such changes in the original spectrogram. This consideration highlights the potential benefit of considering this alternative representation.

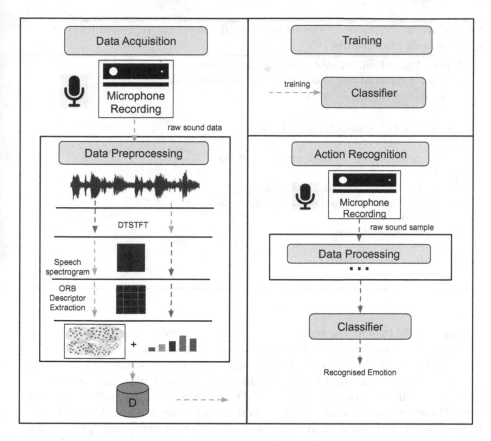

Fig. 2. A visual overview of an abstract version of our methodology. On the right, the representation building procedure is overviewed. From the original audio signal, a spectrogram is produced and ORB descriptors for keypoints arranged in a grid are extracted. A clustering algorithm is executed over all keypoint descriptors, computing a set of clusters corresponding to the visual vocabulary. A soft histogram is then obtained by summing, for each cluster, the soft candidacy scores of keypoints. The produced histogram can be given to a classifier extract emotional content. In this work we propose an attention based neural network classifier. On the left, training and inference are shown. (Figure best viewed in color).

The procedure for constructing the aforementioned representation is given in pseudocode in Procedure 2. The descriptors and vocabulary are obtained following Procedure 1.

Procedure 2. Pseudocode for sequential soft-histogram representation of spectrograms (Taken from [13]).

Input: Data of subsampled audio signals D, parameter set λ;
Result: Sequential soft histogram representation of elements in D;
$\hat{D}$, words $\leftarrow$ Procedure $1(D, \lambda)$;
$seqH \leftarrow \{\}$;
for *each set of descriptors* **d** *in* $\hat{D}$ **do**
$\quad$ seq $\leftarrow$ [ ];
$\quad$ **for** *each column of descriptors* c *in* **d do**
$\quad\quad$ histo $\leftarrow$ **0**;
$\quad\quad$ **for** *each descriptor* d *in* c **do**
$\quad\quad\quad|\quad$ histo $\leftarrow$ histo + soft_score($d, words$);
$\quad\quad$ **end**
$\quad\quad$ seq.append(histo)
$\quad$ **end**
$\quad$ $seqH \leftarrow seqH \cup \{\text{seq}\}$;
end

One way to exploit the temporal structure captured by the described representation, is the use of recurrent neural networks. These models have been widely successful in the task of processing data with a sequential structure and for this reason constitute a natural choice for this task. In particular, [13] propose the use of Long Short-Term Memory (LSTM) networks [55] for emotion classification. These networks utilize "memory" cells, which allow the LSTM architecture to recognise long-term dependencies between sequence items, much more effectively than conventional RNN architectures and other recurrent networks with gated units.

Attention mechanisms have been shown to mitigate the unfavourable compression and loss of information from which typical RNNs suffer even more effectively than LSTMs. In particular, in [9], the authors suggest that recurrent architectures can be entirely replaced by attention mechanisms. We will be particularly interested in so called *self attention* mechanisms. A self attention layer is a sequence-to-sequence mapping which enables us to account for correlations between the input sequence elements, when performing the transformation. In particular, in the simplest situation, every input element is represented by three different vectors, namely, the *query, key* and *value*. To compute the ith output sequence element an attention score is obtained between the ith input sequence element and the rest of the input. An example of an attention scoring function is the, so called, dot product attention which computes the dot product between the ith element query vector and the jth element key vector. Then, a softmax activation is applied on the attention scores to give the attention vector. Finally, the weighted sum of value vectors weighted by attention values is computed to yield the ith output sequence element. In the context of recurrent neural networks, the query vector typically corresponds to RNN hidden states. The idea behind self attention is to convey diverse positions of the same concealed state space originating from the input sequence, based on the case that numerous components together form the overall semantics of a sequence.

Our proposed model utilizes a multi-hop self-attention layer on top of a Bidirectional LSTM layer. The attention layer output is fed into a 2-layer MLP. We use ReLU activation functions throughout the network except for the output layer where softmax activation is used. Dropout layers are used in the model's fully connected layers for regularization purposes and an ℓ_2 penalization term is added to the loss function. A high level visual overview of our model is given in Fig. 3.

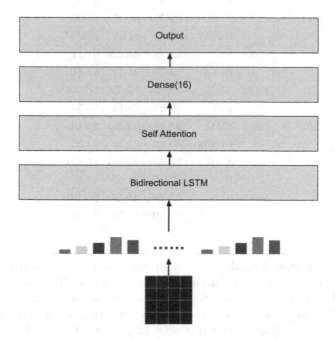

Fig. 3. A visual high-level representation of our proposed network architecture.

4   Experiment Details

This section describes the experiments that were completed for the empirical validation of our approach. For completion, we start by presenting experimental results and procedures from [13], comparing the different BoVW based representations suggested and providing results for the structure preserving method utilizing an LSTM classifier. Next, we perform emotion classification using the attention based neural network proposed in this chapter, over the sequential histogram representation of spectrograms. Moreover, we perform classification experiments using the residual attention network proposed in [28], with the entire spectrogram image as input, as an alternative benchmark.

Table 1. Experimental results comparing soft and hard histogram representations for spectrograms with various shallow classifiers (Taken from [13]).

Dataset	W.C.	Method	SVM	KNN	Random forest
EMO-DB	250	SMH	**47.22**	**50.00**	38.89
		BoVW	44.44	33.33	38.89
	500	SMH	52.78	**41.67**	**52.78**
		BoVW	52.78	38.89	50.00
	1000	SMH	**55.56**	47.50	**55.00**
		BoVW	52.50	47.50	52.50
SAVEE	250	SMH	**31.25**	31.25	25.00
		BoVW	28.13	31.25	25.00
	500	SMH	52.78	**48.89**	61.11
		BoVW	52.78	44.44	61.11
	1000	SMH	**58.33**	**52.78**	**58.33**
		BoVW	55.56	36.11	55.56
EMOVO	250	SMH	**35.00**	**32.50**	**35.00**
		BoVW	30.00	27.50	32.50
	500	SMH	**32.50**	42.50	**35.00**
		BoVW	27.50	27.50	32.50
	1000	SMH	**32.50**	40.00	50.00
		BoVW	27.50	17.50	45.00

For every experiment conducted, visual words were obtained from the spectrograms by running the mini-batch k-means algorithm [33], which offered an effective and efficient clustering option. In more detail, all of the spectrograms were utilized as input for the clustering algorithm to generate the vocabulary, including both the validation and test sets. In practice, this can be done in any setting since no label information is used.

4.1   Dataset Description

The data which we used to run our experiments, consists of the below listed public datasets: EMO-DB [25], SAVEE [27] and EMOVO [26]. The full versions of these datasets contain different emotion labels from one another, and for this reason six labels were selected, common to all three datasets, and only data corresponding to these emotions was used. The emotions considered in our experiments were the following: *Happiness, Sadness, Anger, Fear* and *Neutral*. For each dataset, each sample was truncated to be of length 2 s, and the DTSTFT was performed with parameters $T_S = 20$ ms and $T_W = 40$ ms to produce a spectrogram. In turn, for each spectrogram, a 50-by-50 equidistant grid of keypoints was defined over the entire image with three scale parameters leading to 7500 descriptors per recording. For the keypoints, 128-feature orb descriptors were used.

4.2   Experimental Procedure Description

Firstly, an evaluation of the soft histogram representation against the typical hard histogram representation is presented as carried out in [13]. To this end, three popular shallow classifiers were utilized: SVM (with an RBF kernel), Random Forest and k-nearest neighbors where the Euclidean distance was chosen as a distance measure. Different proximity measures where also tested for the k-nearest neighbor classifier, including ℓ_1 and Wasserstein distance but we empirically found that the results were not as good. Each classifier was trained on different data representations and the test accuracy was used a measure of fitness for these representations.

The train-test split was chosen to be 90%–10% for each dataset. For *each* representation, hyperparameters were selected through grid search and 5-folds stratified cross validation. The best performing hyperparameters among all folds were chosen as the best. The resulting classifier was trained on the entire training set, and the test accuracy was reported. The entire evaluation process was repeated for three different numbers of visual word. These were 250, 500 and 1000. The results are reported in Table 1, as taken from [13].

Similarly, we report the results obtained by analyzing the sequential histogram representation of spectrograms using the LSTM. Again, for each dataset the same three different word counts are used as before. Ten models are trained on ten different random train-validation-test splits, with respective percentages 80%, 10% and 10%. The validation set is used to perform early stopping regularization. The maximum, minimum and mean test accuracies are reported for each dataset and word count combination. The results are summarized in Table 2, as taken from [13].

Table 2. Results for the LSTM classification experiment. Accuracies are given in percentages, W.C. represents word count and B represents the benchmark obtained from shallow classifiers presented in Table 1 (Taken from [13]).

Dataset	W.C.	Accuracy			B
		Mean	Max	Min	
EMO-DB	250	**59.76**	60.98	58.54	50.00
	500	**62.93**	63.17	60.54	52.78
	1000	**56.48**	57.34	56.10	55.56
SAVEE	250	**37.77**	44.44	30.55	31.25
	500	**65.08**	69.16	62.22	61.11
	1000	**68.77**	70.55	66.39	58.33
EMOVO	250	**40.91**	42.86	38.90	35.00
	500	**50.98**	57.14	47.62	42.50
	1000	**50.12**	53.64	46.53	50.00

To serve as a benchmark we further conducted an experiment where we used a residual attention network on the entire spectrogram image. A train-validation-test random split was performed, again with percentages 80%, 10% and 10%. An earlystopping callback was utilized, monitoring the validation set loss value with a patience parameter set to 5. The test set accuracy and f1 score were measured and the entire process was repeated 10 times. The average metrics from these runs are reported in Table 3.

Table 3. Results of evaluating the residual attention network directly on the spectrogram images. The results are represented in percentages and correspond to mean test set metrics over 10 runs.

Dataset	Accuracy	F1 score
EMO-DB	59.49	58.32
SAVEE	36.11	11.88
EMOVO	35.00	34.12

Finally, we perform an experiment to evaluate the performance of our proposed attention-based recurrent neural network on the sequential soft histogram representation of the spectrograms. A similar procedure to above was used with an 80% − 10% − 10% train-validation-test split, using an early stopping callback with patience 5. For each dataset, three different vocabulary sizes, namely 250, 500 and 1000 were used, in accordance with previous experiments. The mean metric scores are reported for each of 10 different runs. The results are summarized in Tables 4, 5 and 6.

Table 4. Results for the proposed attention-based neural network classification experiment with a vocabulary size of 250. Metrics are given in percentages.

Dataset	Accuracy	F1 score
EMO-DB	51.27	39.08
SAVEE	37.81	32.84
EMOVO	40.97	27.14

Table 5. Results for the proposed attention-based neural network classification experiment with a vocabulary size of 500. Metrics are given in percentages.

Dataset	Accuracy	F1 score
EMO-DB	63.18	58.11
SAVEE	68.01	64.17
EMOVO	54.69	53.12

Table 6. Results for the proposed attention-based neural network classification experiment with a vocabulary size of 1000. Metrics are given in percentages.

Dataset	Accuracy	F1 score
EMO-DB	63.21	61.95
SAVEE	57.51	51.24
EMOVO	50.99	50.03

5 Discussion on Results

The produced results are aligned with what we expected, while we can also make some interesting observations. Firstly, it is observed that using a soft histogram representation instead of a conventional BoVW model indeed yields better performing classifiers. This is intuitive since soft histograms make up richer representations in lower dimensionalities, i.e. for smaller vocabulary sizes. Moreover, we observe that the number of visual words used plays an important role in the accuracy of produced classifiers for both representations. While we see that 250 words usually yield worse classifiers than both 500 and 1000 words, 500 words often outperform 1000 words. This indicates that while 250 words are often too few, significantly under representing the spectrogram, it is often the case that 1000 words are too many, yielding a too high dimensional representation. In practice, the number of keywords should be selected using some validation technique.

We further note, as expected that, the temporal structure preserving representation given by sequences of histograms provides much better classification results when combined with sequence processing models. In particular, the LSTMs that were trained on these representation significantly outperform the shallow classifiers obtained by the simple soft histogram representations. This can also be contrasted with the residual attention network which was trained on the raw spectrogram images. We see that this performed much worse than the LSTM. Moreover, even though it achieved relatively good results on EMO-DB, it significantly under performed on the other two datasets.

Finally, the attention based sequence processing model proved to be very effective. Indeed, for most setups it produced comparable or better results than the plain LSTM. Again, we make the same observations regarding the number of words and in practice this hyperparameter should be tuned through validation.

6 Closing Remarks

Recently, interest in emotion recognition research has increased, especially over sound, as it is important in many human-computer interaction applications and sound recordings can be collected without causing discomfort to individuals as alternative methods such as video or body sensor readings. In this chapter, we have discussed some novel methods for the analysis of the emotional content of audio signals obtained from vocalized speech, using the classification paradigm for sentiment analysis. In particular, we reviewed dimensionality reduction techniques for speech spectrograms which rely on BoVW models and introduced an attention based neural network model for analyzing such representations.

The explored approaches offer good performance and can be found useful in various applications, like assisted living and personalized content suggestion. In addition, our methods process sound data, the collection of which is considered least invasive amongst other alternatives and this makes our approach a good candidate for potential implementations of ER capable systems. Moreover, because our method is non-linguistic, relying on low-level audio features (spectrograms), it leads to models that are not dependent on language. We experimentally verified our method's good performance on data in English and German.

After extensive experimentation, we empirically validated our methods and drew the following conclusions. Firstly, our BoVW dimensionality reduction technique offer an effective and efficient method for constructing concise representations of speech signals for analysing sentiment. We found that preserving the structure of the spectrogram in the extracted representation is beneficial for the classification task, and that our sequential histogram representation in combination with either recurrent neural networks or attention-based networks offers classifiers with very satisfactory performance. We found that attention-based networks are particularly well suited for the emotion recognition task, especially when combined with our concise representation of spectrograms. In particular, we conclude that the approaches suggested here offer a significantly outperform previous work that utilizes BoVW representations.

References

1. Cowie, R., et al.: Emotion recognition in human-computer interaction. IEEE Sign. Process. Mag. **18**(1), 32–80 (2001)
2. Poria, S., Chaturvedi, I., Cambria, E., Hussain, A.: Convolutional MKL based multimodal emotion recognition and sentiment analysis. In: 2016 IEEE 16th International Conference on Data Mining (ICDM), pp. 439–448. IEEE (2016)
3. Zeng, E., Mare, S., Roesner, F.: End user security and privacy concerns with smart homes. In Thirteenth Symposium on Usable Privacy and Security (SOUPS 2017), pp. 65–80 (2017)
4. Sauter, D.A., Eisner, F., Calder, A.J., Scott, S.K.: Perceptual cues in nonverbal vocal expressions of emotion. Quart. J. Exp. Psychol. **63**(11), 2251–2272 (2010)
5. Anagnostopoulos, C.N., Iliou, T., Giannoukos, I.: Features and classifiers for emotion recognition from speech: a survey from 2000 to 2011. Artif. Intell. Rev. **43**(2), 155–177 (2015). https://doi.org/10.1007/s10462-012-9368-5
6. El Ayadi, M., Kamel, M.S., Karray, F.: Survey on speech emotion recognition: features, classification schemes, and databases. Pattern Recogn. **44**(3), 572–587 (2011)
7. Giannakopoulos, T., Pikrakis, A.: Introduction to Audio Analysis: A MATLAB® Approach. Academic Press, Cambridge (2014)

8. Drakopoulos, G., Pikramenos, G., Spyrou, E.D., Perantonis, S.J.: Emotion recognition from speech: a survey. In: WEBIST, pp. 432–439 (2019)
9. Vaswani, A., et al.: Attention is all you need. In: Advances in Neural Information Processing Systems, pp. 5998–6008 (2017)
10. Badshah, A.M., Ahmad, J., Rahim, N., Baik, S.W.: Speech emotion recognition from spectrograms with deep convolutional neural network. In: 2017 International Conference on Platform Technology and Service (PlatCon), pp. 1–5. IEEE (2017)
11. Satt, A., Rozenberg, S., Hoory, R.: Efficient emotion recognition from speech using deep learning on spectrograms (2017)
12. He, L., Lech, M., Maddage, N., Allen, N.: Stress and emotion recognition using log-Gabor filter analysis of speech spectrograms. In 2009 3rd International Conference on Affective Computing and Intelligent Interaction and Workshops, pp. 1–6. IEEE (2009)
13. Pikramenos, G., Smyrnis, G., Vernikos, I., Konidaris, T., Spyrou, E., Perantonis, S.J.: Sentiment analysis from sound spectrograms via soft BoVW and temporal structure modelling. In: ICPRAM, pp. 361–369 (2020)
14. Lim, W., Jang, D., Lee, T.: Speech emotion recognition using convolutional and recurrent neural networks. In: 2016 Asia-Pacific Signal and Information Processing Association Annual Summit and Conference (APSIPA), pp. 1–4. IEEE (2016)
15. Wang, Y., Guan, L.: Recognizing human emotional state from audiovisual signals. IEEE Trans. Multimedia **10**(5), 936–946 (2008)
16. Nogueiras, A., Moreno, A., Bonafonte, A., & Mariño, J. B.: Speech emotion recognition using hidden Markov models. In Seventh European Conference on Speech Communication and Technology (2001)
17. Spyrou, E., Nikopoulou, R., Vernikos, I., Mylonas, P.: Emotion recognition from speech using the bag-of-visual words on audio segment spectrograms. Technologies **7**(1), 20 (2019)
18. Hanjalic, A.: Extracting moods from pictures and sounds: Towards truly personalized TV. IEEE Sign. Process. Mag. **23**(2), 90–100 (2006)
19. Rozgić, V., Ananthakrishnan, S., Saleem, S., Kumar, R., Vembu, A.N., Prasad, R.: Emotion recognition using acoustic and lexical features. In Thirteenth Annual Conference of the International Speech Communication Association (2012)
20. Rublee, E., Rabaud, V., Konolige, K., Bradski, G.: ORB: an efficient alternative to SIFT or SURF. In: 2011 International Conference on Computer Vision, pp. 2564–2571. IEEE (2011)
21. Hu, D.: An introductory survey on attention mechanisms in NLP problems. In: Bi, Y., Bhatia, R., Kapoor, S. (eds.) IntelliSys 2019. AISC, vol. 1038, pp. 432–448. Springer, Cham (2020). https://doi.org/10.1007/978-3-030-29513-4_31
22. Kristensen, L.B., Wang, L., Petersson, K.M., Hagoort, P.: The interface between language and attention: prosodic focus marking recruits a general attention network in spoken language comprehension. Cereb. Cortex **23**(8), 1836–1848 (2013)
23. Galassi, A., Lippi, M., Torroni, P.: Attention, please! a critical review of neural attention models in natural language processing. arXiv preprint. arXiv:1902.02181 (2019)
24. Mao, Q., Dong, M., Huang, Z., Zhan, Y.: Learning salient features for speech emotion recognition using convolutional neural networks. IEEE Trans. Multimedia **16**(8), 2203–2213 (2014)
25. Burkhardt, F., Paeschke, A., Rolfes, M., Sendlmeier, W. F., Weiss, B.: A database of German emotional speech. In Ninth European Conference on Speech Communication and Technology (2005)

26. Costantini, G., Iaderola, I., Paoloni, A., Todisco, M.: EMOVO corpus: an Italian emotional speech database. In: International Conference on Language Resources and Evaluation (LREC 2014), pp. 3501–3504. European Language Resources Association (ELRA) (2014)

27. Jackson, P., Haq, S.: Surrey audio-visual expressed emotion (SAVEE) database. University of Surrey, Guildford, UK (2014)

28. Wang, F., Jiang, M., Qian, C., Yang, S., Li, C., Zhang, H., Tang, X.: Residual attention network for image classification. In: Proceedings of the IEEE Conference on Computer Vision and Pattern Recognition, pp. 3156–3164 (2017)

29. Salazar, J., Kirchhoff, K., Huang, Z.: Self-attention networks for connectionist temporal classification in speech recognition. In: ICASSP 2019–2019 IEEE International Conference on Acoustics, Speech and Signal Processing (ICASSP), pp. 7115–7119. IEEE (2019)

30. Lin, Z., Feng, M., Santos, C.N.D., Yu, M., Xiang, B., Zhou, B., Bengio, Y.: A structured self-attentive sentence embedding. arXiv preprint. arXiv:1703.03130 (2017)

31. Yan, Z., Liu, W., Wen, S., Yang, Y.: Multi-label image classification by feature attention network. IEEE Access **7**, 98005–98013 (2019)

32. Mehrabian, A.: Framework for a comprehensive description and measurement of emotional states. Genet. Soc. Gen. Psychol. Monogr. 121, 339–361 (1995)

33. Sculley, D.: Web-scale k-means clustering. In: Proceedings of the 19th International Conference on World Wide Web, pp. 1177–1178 (2010)

34. Binali, H., Wu, C., Potdar, V.: Computational approaches for emotion detection in text. In: 4th IEEE International Conference on Digital Ecosystems and Technologies, pp. 172–177. IEEE (2010)

35. Jin, Q., Li, C., Chen, S., Wu, H.: Speech emotion recognition with acoustic and lexical features. In 2015 IEEE International Conference on Acoustics, Speech and Signal Processing (ICASSP), pp. 4749–4753. IEEE (2015)

36. Lu, L., Liu, D., Zhang, H.J.: Automatic mood detection and tracking of music audio signals. IEEE Trans. Audio Speech Lang. Process. **14**(1), 5–18 (2005)

37. Yang, Y.H., Lin, Y.C., Su, Y.F., Chen, H.H.: A regression approach to music emotion recognition. IEEE Trans. Audio Speech Lang. Process. **16**(2), 448–457 (2008)

38. Panda, R., Malheiro, R.M., Paiva, R.P.: Novel audio features for music emotion recognition. IEEE Trans. Affect. Comput. 11, 614–626 (2018)

39. Grimm, M., Kroschel, K., Mower, E., Narayanan, S.: Primitives-based evaluation and estimation of emotions in speech. Speech Commun. **49**(10–11), 787–800 (2007)

40. Lowe, D.G.: Distinctive image features from scale-invariant keypoints. Int. J. Comput. Vis. **60**(2), 91–110 (2004). https://doi.org/10.1023/B:VISI.0000029664.99615.94

41. Bay, H., Tuytelaars, T., Van Gool, L.: SURF: speeded up robust features. In: Leonardis, A., Bischof, H., Pinz, A. (eds.) ECCV 2006. LNCS, vol. 3951, pp. 404–417. Springer, Heidelberg (2006). https://doi.org/10.1007/11744023_32

42. Wöllmer, M., et al.: Abandoning emotion classes-towards continuous emotion recognition with modelling of long-range dependencies. In: Proceedings of the 9th Interspeech 2008 Incorp. 12th Australasian International Conference on Speech Science and Technology SST 2008, Brisbane, Australia, pp. 597–600 (2008)

43. Giannakopoulos, T., Pikrakis, A., Theodoridis, S.: A dimensional approach to emotion recognition of speech from movies. In: 2009 IEEE International Conference on Acoustics, Speech and Signal Processing, pp. 65–68. IEEE (2009)

44. Lee, H., Pham, P., Largman, Y., Ng, A.Y.: Unsupervised feature learning for audio classification using convolutional deep belief networks. In: Advances in Neural Information Processing Systems, pp. 1096–1104 (2009)
45. Zhang, T., Kuo, C.C.J.: Audio content analysis for online audiovisual data segmentation and classification. IEEE Trans. Speech Audio Process. **9**(4), 441–457 (2001)
46. Busso, C., et al.: IEMOCAP: interactive emotional dyadic motion capture database. Lang. Resour. Eval. **42**(4), 335 (2008)
47. Plutchik, R.: A general psychoevolutionary theory of emotion. In: Theories of Emotion, pp. 3–33. Academic press, Cambridge (1980)
48. Papakostas, M., et al.: Deep visual attributes vs. hand-crafted audio features on multidomain speech emotion recognition. Computation **5**(2), 26 (2017)
49. Martiínez, J.G.: Recognition and emotions. A critical approach on education. Procedia Soc. Behav. Sci. **46**, 3925–3930 (2012)
50. Tickle, A., Raghu, S., Elshaw, M.: Emotional recognition from the speech signal for a virtual education agent. J. Phys. Conf. Ser. **450**(1), 012053 (2013)
51. Bahreini, K., Nadolski, R., Westera, W.: Towards real-time speech emotion recognition for affective e-learning. Educ. Inf. Technol. **21**(5), 1367–1386 (2016). https://doi.org/10.1007/s10639-015-9388-2
52. Busso, C., et al.: Analysis of emotion recognition using facial expressions, speech and multimodal information. In: Proceedings of the 6th International Conference on Multimodal Interfaces, pp. 205–211 (2004)
53. Wöllmer, M., Metallinou, A., Eyben, F., Schuller, B., Narayanan, S.: Context-sensitive multimodal emotion recognition from speech and facial expression using bidirectional LSTM modeling. In: Proceedings of the INTERSPEECH 2010, Makuhari, Japan, pp. 2362–2365 (2010)
54. Trentin, E., Scherer, S., Schwenker, F.: Emotion recognition from speech signals via a probabilistic echo-state network. Pattern Recogn. Lett. **66**, 4–12 (2015)
55. Hochreiter, S., Schmidhuber, J.: Long short-term memory. Neural Comput. **9**(8), 1735–1780 (1997)
56. Sak, H., Senior, A.W., Beaufays, F.: Long short-term memory recurrent neural network architectures for large scale acoustic modeling (2014)
57. Theodoridis, S., Koutroumbas, K.: Pattern recognition and neural networks. In: Paliouras, G., Karkaletsis, V., Spyropoulos, C.D. (eds.) ACAI 1999. LNCS (LNAI), vol. 2049, pp. 169–195. Springer, Heidelberg (2001). https://doi.org/10.1007/3-540-44673-7_8
58. Aminbeidokhti, M., Pedersoli, M., Cardinal, P., Granger, E.: Emotion recognition with spatial attention and temporal softmax pooling. In: Karray, F., Campilho, A., Yu, A. (eds.) ICIAR 2019. LNCS, vol. 11662, pp. 323–331. Springer, Cham (2019). https://doi.org/10.1007/978-3-030-27202-9_29
59. Gupta, A., Agrawal, D., Chauhan, H., Dolz, J., Pedersoli, M.: An attention model for group-level emotion recognition. In: Proceedings of the 20th ACM International Conference on Multimodal Interaction, pp. 611–615 (2018)
60. Tarantino, L., Garner, P.N., Lazaridis, A.: Self-Attention for speech emotion recognition. In: INTERSPEECH, pp. 2578–2582 (2019)

Efficient Radial Distortion Correction
for Planar Motion

Marcus Valtonen Örnhag[(⊠)]

Centre for Mathematical Sciences, Lund University, Lund, Sweden
marcus.valtonen_ornhag@math.lth.se

Abstract. In this paper we investigate simultaneous radial distortion calibration and motion estimation for vehicles travelling parallel to planar surfaces. This is done by estimating the inter-image homography between two poses, as well as the distortion parameter. Radial distortion correction is often performed as a pre-calibration step; however, accurately estimating the distortion profile without special scene requirements may make such procedures obsolete. As many modern day consumer cameras are affected by radial distortion to some degree, there is a great potential to reduce production time, if properly implemented.

We devise two polynomial solvers, for radially distorted homographies compatible with different models of planar motion. We show that the algorithms are numerically stable, and sufficiently fast to be incorporated in a real-time frameworks. Furthermore, we show on both synthetic and real data, that the proposed solvers perform well compared to competing methods.

Keywords: Radial distortion correction · Homography · Visual odometry · Polynomial solvers

1 Introduction

When designing a Visual Odometry (VO) pipeline it is beneficial to integrate any prior knowledge of the intended environment or known motion model parameters. One particular instance, that will be further investigated in this paper, is the planar motion model, in which a vehicle travels on—or parallel to—a planar surface. Such a scenario is common in man-made environments, but can also accurately approximate outdoor scenarios under certain conditions, such as cars travelling on a highway. In the current literature we find several papers on planar motion models, restricted to fit particular use cases or pre-calibrated parameters [3,6,20]. The general case, however, was first introduced in [17] which

The author gratefully acknowledges Mårten Wadenbäck and Martin Karlsson for providing the data for the planar motion compatible sequences, and Magnus Oskarsson for fruitful discussions regarding the basis selection heuristic which made the proposed solvers faster. This work has been funded by the Swedish Research Council through grant no. 2015-05639 'Visual SLAM based on Planar Homographies'.

M. De Marsico et al. (Eds.): ICPRAM 2020, LNCS 12594, pp. 46–63, 2020.
https://doi.org/10.1007/978-3-030-66125-0_4

incorporates two unknown overhead tilt angles, which are assumed to be constant throughout the trajectory of the vehicle. They assumed the floor is in the field of view of the camera, allowing them to compute the motion parameters through inter-image homographies. Another approach utilizing the floor to compute the motions was done by [6]. More recent development was done by [26,27], and is the first to accurately recover the complete set of motion parameters using inter-image homographies. Other notable approaches include that of [30], in which a planar VO pipeline using a dense matching scheme was proposed.

In the most general setting, assuming the camera is rigidly mounted on the vehicle, the number of motion parameters are reduced to five, which should be compared to the general homography, which has eight degrees of freedom [7]. These parameters consist of the two overhead tilt parameters, and three non-constant parameters: one rotational angle (about the floor normal), and two translational components.

In order to obtain a homography, keypoints are extracted and matched. These keypoints then serve as input to the homography estimation algorithm. Since the extraction and matching steps are imperfect for any realistic image sequence, outliers and noise are prone to exist. Typical steps taken to resolve this issue include the use of robust estimation frameworks, e.g. RANSAC. It is at this point the benefit of working with fewer motion parameters come to light. Since fewer motion parameters demand fewer point correspondences in order to be estimated, one can select a minimal amount of points in the RANSAC framework. The fewer points you are able to select, the greater the probability of selecting only inliers. By doing so, one can reduce the number of RANSAC iterations.

In the general case, with four point correspondences, one may linearly extract the homography; however, if any of the motion parameters are known or constrained, this may no longer be the case, as the resulting systems of equations often are nonlinear. This poses a new type of problem—can we solve these equations sufficiently fast and accurate? Luckily, many methods from computational algebraic geometry [4] has been used in many computer vision problems, and certain frameworks already exist for how to proceed. One of the earliest, and still used today, was [9].

This paper is a revised journal version of [25], where we will consider the general planar motion model with unknown radial distortion, and devise a polynomial solver that can accurately recover the motion and distortion parameters in real-time applications. Furthermore, we propose a planar motion compatible minimal two point solver with radial distortion when the tilt angles are known. This situation arises when the tilt is pre-calibrated or can be accessed using external sensors, such as an IMU to extract the gravity direction. For indoor scenarios, assuming that the gravity direction is aligned with the floor normal—which often is a valid approximation—is equivalent to knowing the tilt angles. There are situations where similar assumptions can be made, without significant loss in accuracy, e.g. aerial imagery. Regardless of the situation, radial distortion is necessary to account for in any accurate VO pipeline, and is often done in a pre-calibration step, where the distortion parameters are obtained. By incorporating the parameter in the homography estimation process, we hope to eliminate this pre-processing step.

2   Related Work

2.1   Homography Estimation

The *Direct Linear Transform* (DLT) equations is a linear system of equations to extract a homography H given a number of point correspondences. In the general setting, with eight degrees of freedom, the minimal case requires four point correspondences. To see this, let us consider a single pair of point correspondences on a common scene plane, denoted by $x \leftrightarrow \hat{x}$. They are related by a homography H as $\lambda\hat{x} = Hx$, for some scalar $\lambda \neq 0$. Equivalently, we may express this as $\hat{x} \times Hx = 0$, thus eliminating the scale parameter λ, or,

$$\begin{bmatrix} 0 & -\hat{w}x^T & \hat{y}x^T \\ \hat{w}x^T & 0 & -\hat{x}x^T \\ -\hat{y}x^T & \hat{x}x^T & 0 \end{bmatrix} \begin{bmatrix} h_1 \\ h_2 \\ h_3 \end{bmatrix} = 0, \tag{1}$$

assuming homogeneous coordinates, i.e. $x \doteq [x, y, w]^T$ and $\hat{x} = [\hat{x}, \hat{y}, \hat{w}]^T$, respectively. Here h_k^T is the k:th row of the homography matrix H. As the cross product introduces a linear dependence, only two of the equations are necessary, hence explaining why four point correspondences are minimal in the general case. Thus, using four point correspondences the problem can be transformed into finding the one-dimensional null space $h = [h_1^T \ h_2^T \ h_3^T]^T$, which is typically obtained using SVD of the coefficient matrix.

In the general planar motion model there are only five motion parameters, hence the minimal case requires but 2.5 point correspondences. Similarly, we may construct a system of equations, by using three point correspondences and discard the last equation in the corresponding DLT system. This can be written as $Ch = 0$ where $C \in \mathbb{R}^{5\times9}$ is the coefficient matrix. Again, this is a problem of finding the null space of C; however, the null space is now four-dimensional. As an additional step, one must now find the null space coefficients which makes H a homography compatible with the general planar motion model. It was shown in [24, 29] that there are eleven quartic constraints (as well as a sextic constraint) in the elements of H that has to be fulfilled in order to guarantee compatibility.

2.2   Modelling Radial Distortion

In order to compensate for the radial distortion, several models have been proposed. A classic method, still in use today, is the Brown–Conrady model [2], in which also tangential distortion is corrected. The division model introduced in [5], has gained attention as it provides accurate approximations of the distortion profile with fewer parameters. For this reason, we will only consider the distortion model, and restrict ourselves to a single distortion parameter, as this allows us to use fewer point correspondences.

Let λ denote the distortion parameter. Then the distorted (or measured) image points can be expressed as $\boldsymbol{x}_i = [x_i, y_i, 1]^T$

$$\boldsymbol{x}_i^u = f(\boldsymbol{x}_i, \lambda) = \begin{bmatrix} x_i \\ y_i \\ 1 + \lambda(x_i^2 + y_i^2) \end{bmatrix}, \tag{2}$$

where $\boldsymbol{x}_i^u$ are the undistorted image points, assuming the distortion center is aligned to the center of the image. Furthermore, we select the coordinate system such that the origin is aligned with the distortion center.

We may now modify the DLT equations (1) as the distortion parameter only appears in the homogeneous coordinates. Consider two point correspondences $\boldsymbol{x}_i \leftrightarrow \hat{\boldsymbol{x}}_i$, then

$$f(\hat{\boldsymbol{x}}_i, \lambda) \times \boldsymbol{H} f(\boldsymbol{x}_i, \lambda) = \boldsymbol{0} . \tag{3}$$

This approach has been used for the general case of radially distorted homographies [11], conjugate translations with radial distortion [21], and the case of jointly estimating lens distortion and affine rectification from coplanar features [22]. The last two use an explicit parameterization of the motion parameters, instead of trying to parameterize the null space of the DLT system. In common for all methods is that the resulting problem is a polynomial system of equations, and is solved by further reduction to an eigenvalue problem [4]. Automatic solvers for polynomial systems have been proposed, primarily using Gröbner bases, such as [9,12–14,16], or resultant based methods [1]. Alternative approaches include considering the problem as a Quadratic Eigenvalue Problem (QEP) [5,8,10].

3   The General Planar Motion Model

Consider a camera mounted rigidly on a vehicle travelling on a planar surface. We model this scenario by assuming that the camera moves in the plane $z = 0$, parallel to the surface on which the vehicle moves, located in $z = 1$. This parameterization also fixes the scale of the global coordinate system.

Consider two consecutive views, A and B, with the corresponding camera matrices

$$\begin{aligned} \boldsymbol{P}_A &= \boldsymbol{R}_{\psi\theta}[\boldsymbol{I} \mid \boldsymbol{0}], \\ \boldsymbol{P}_B &= \boldsymbol{R}_{\psi\theta}\boldsymbol{R}_\phi[\boldsymbol{I} \mid -\boldsymbol{t}], \end{aligned} \tag{4}$$

where the constant overhead tilt is modeled by $\boldsymbol{R}_{\psi\theta}$, and consists of a rotation θ about the y-axis followed by a rotation of ψ about the x-axis. Furthermore, we allow the vehicle to rotate an angle ϕ about the z-axis, which may vary. As the camera is assumed to be mounted rigidly on the vehicle, the height above the floor is constant, hence we may assume that it travels in the plane $z = 0$, leaving two translation components t_x and t_y, see Fig. 1. From this, one may derive the corresponding inter-image homography

$$\boldsymbol{H} = \lambda \boldsymbol{R}_{\psi\theta} \boldsymbol{R}_\phi \boldsymbol{T}_t \boldsymbol{R}_{\psi\theta}^T, \tag{5}$$

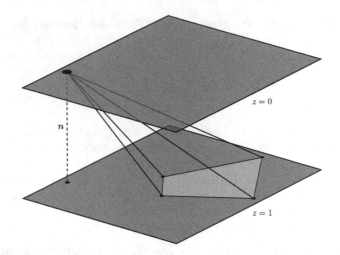

Fig. 1. Illustration of the problem geometry considered in the paper. The camera is mounted rigidly on a mobile platform, thus travelling parallel to the ground floor in the plane $z = 0$. We allow a constant, but generally unknown, overhead tilt to be present, which is modelled by the angles psi (about the x-axis and θ (about the y-axis). Furthermore, the camera can rotate about the z-axis (by an angle ϕ) and translate in the plane $z = 0$, i.e. there are in total five degrees of freedom—three rotations and two translations. Figure reproduced from [25].

where $\boldsymbol{T_t} = \boldsymbol{I} - \boldsymbol{t}\boldsymbol{n}^T$ is a translation matrix, for the translation $\boldsymbol{t} = [t_x, t_y, 0]^T$, relative the plane normal $\boldsymbol{n} = [0, 0, 1]^T$. The homography matrix can be made unique by e.g. imposing $\det(\boldsymbol{H}) = 1$.

In addition to the DLT constraints, the elements of a homography compatible with the general planar motion model must satisfy a number of polynomial constraints. Such constraints were numerically derived in [29], where it was shown that that there are at least eleven quartic constraints. The novel theoretical framework used in [24], showed that these constraints were necessary, but not sufficient; however, by adding a sextic constraint, it was shown that they are sufficient.

4 Polynomial Solvers

4.1 A Non-minimal Relaxation (4 Point)

In theory, one would be able to construct a minimal solver with three point correspondences, as there are six degrees of freedom—the five motion parameters discussed in Sect. 3, and the distortion parameter. In practice, however, this problem is hard, and we have yet to find a tractable solution which is numerically stable and sufficiently fast for real-time applications. Consequently, we have opted for a non-minimal four point relaxation. We do believe this is an acceptable compromise, as a general homography with a single distortion parameter requires 4.5 point correspondences for the minimal configuration. This effectively means one has to sample five point pairs to estimate a hypothesis. This section is largely reproduced from [25].

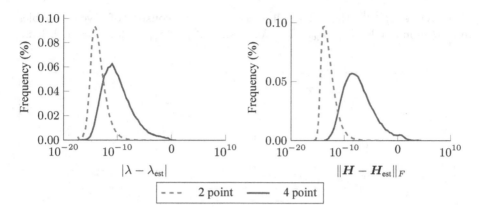

Fig. 2. Error histogram of the estimated distortion parameter λ (left) and the homography H for 100,000 random instances, for both of the proposed methods.

Similarly, to the approach in [11] we expand the third row of (3); however, we consider using only four point correspondences. This results in the following equation

$$(-\hat{y}_i h_{11} + \hat{x}_i h_{21})x_i + (-\hat{y}_i h_{12} + \hat{x}_i h_{22})y_i + (-\hat{y}_i h_{13} + \hat{x}_i h_{23})w_i = 0, \quad (6)$$

where $w_i = 1 + \lambda(x_i^2 + y_i^2)$ and $\hat{w}_i = 1 + \lambda(\hat{x}_i^2 + \hat{y}_i^2)$ are functions of the radial distortion parameter λ. There are eight monomials involved in this expression, namely

$$v_1 = \begin{bmatrix} h_{11} & h_{12} & h_{13} & h_{21} & h_{22} & h_{23} & \lambda h_{13} & \lambda h_{23} \end{bmatrix}^T. \quad (7)$$

Using four point correspondences results in a system of equations, which can be written as

$$M_1 v_1 = 0, \quad (8)$$

where M_1 is a 4×8 matrix. For non-degenerate configurations the null space of M_1 is four-dimensional. Consequently, we may parameterize v_1 as

$$v_1 = \sum_{i=1}^{4} \gamma_i n_i, \quad (9)$$

where γ_i are unknown basis coefficients. Since the last two monomials of v_1 depend on the previous elements, this relation has to be enforced when computing the basis coefficients γ_i. These give rise to two equations

$$v_8 = \lambda v_6 \quad \text{and} \quad v_7 = \lambda v_3. \quad (10)$$

Furthermore, we proceed to fix the scale by letting $\gamma_4 = 1$.

We will now use the second row of (3). Similarly, we may write this as

$$M_2 v_2 = 0, \tag{11}$$

where $M_2 \in \mathbb{R}^{4 \times 16}$. Here the null space vector v_2 consists of seven variables, and 16 monomials: h_{31}, h_{32}, h_{33}, λh_{33} and $\lambda^2 \gamma_i$, $\lambda \gamma_i$, γ_i for $i = 1, 2, 3$ and

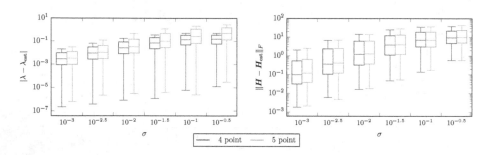

Fig. 3. Distribution of estimation error in the distortion parameter λ, and the homography H (measured in the Frobenius norm) for different noise levels σ and unknown tilt. The proposed solver is compared to the five point solver [5]. Figure and caption reproduced from [25].

λ^2, λ, 1. We may now proceed to eliminate the first three variables—h_{31}, h_{32} and h_{33}—as they are only present in four monomials. As we are using four point correspondences, yielding four equations, Gauss–Jordan elimination can be used. We obtain the following upon performing the elimination

$$\hat{M}_2 = \begin{array}{c} \\ \end{array} \overset{\displaystyle h_{31}\ h_{32}\ \lambda h_{33}\ h_{33}\ \lambda^2 \gamma_1\ \lambda \gamma_1\ \gamma_1 \qquad \lambda^2\ \lambda\ 1}{\begin{bmatrix} 1 & & & & \bullet & \bullet & \bullet & \cdots & \bullet & \bullet & \bullet \\ & 1 & & & \bullet & \bullet & \bullet & \cdots & \bullet & \bullet & \bullet \\ & & 1 & & \bullet & \bullet & \bullet & \cdots & \bullet & \bullet & \bullet \\ & & & 1 & \bullet & \bullet & \bullet & \cdots & \bullet & \bullet & \bullet \end{bmatrix}} . \tag{12}$$

It turns out that the columns of the right 4×12 submatrix are not independent. In order to generate a correct solver, it is important to generate integer instances satisfying these dependencies.

From the eliminated system $\hat{M}_2 v_2 = 0$ we get the four equations

$$\begin{aligned} h_{31} + f_1(\gamma_1, \gamma_2, \gamma_3, \lambda) &= 0, \\ h_{32} + f_2(\gamma_1, \gamma_2, \gamma_3, \lambda) &= 0, \\ \lambda h_{33} + f_3(\gamma_1, \gamma_2, \gamma_3, \lambda) &= 0, \\ h_{33} + f_4(\gamma_1, \gamma_2, \gamma_3, \lambda) &= 0, \end{aligned} \tag{13}$$

where $f_i(\gamma_1, \gamma_2, \gamma_3, \lambda)$ are polynomials in the variables γ_1, γ_2, γ_3, λ. Exploiting the relations between the last two equations of (13), an additional constraint is obtained

$$\lambda f_4(\gamma_1, \gamma_2, \gamma_3, \lambda) = f_3(\gamma_1, \gamma_2, \gamma_3, \lambda) . \tag{14}$$

The eliminated variables h_{31}, h_{32} and h_{33} are polynomials of degree three, thus making (14) of degree four. Together with (10) we have three equations in four unknowns. Since we are able to express all elements of the homography H as a function of four variables, we can enforce one of the 11 quartic constraints originally found in [29]. Evaluating these constraints using H it turns out that ten of the constraints are of degree 12 and one of degree 10 due to cancellation of higher order terms. We choose the smallest one to build the polynomial solver.

Using the automatic generator [12] we find that there are 18 solutions to the problem in general, and by sampling a basis based on the heuristic presented in [15] an elimination template of size 177×195 could be created.

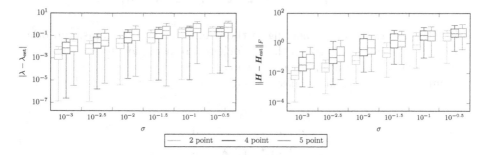

Fig. 4. Distribution of estimation error in the distortion parameter λ, and the homography H (measured in the Frobenius norm) for different noise levels σ and known tilt (assumed to be compensated for). The proposed two point solver is compared to the four point and five point solver [5]. Distribution of estimation error in the distortion parameter λ, and the homography H (measured in the Frobenius norm) for different noise levels σ and known tilt (assumed to be compensated for). The proposed two point solver is compared to the four point and five point solver [5].

4.2 Minimal Solver with Known Tilt (2 Point)

If the tilt angles are known, we can treat the planar motion case with radial distortion. In this case there are four degrees of freedom, and thus the minimal configuration requires two point correspondences. In this section, we will derive a novel solver for this case. Using a different approach than in the previous section, we may explicitly parameterize the homography. Let us use the following parameterization for the rotation matrix

$$
R_z = \begin{bmatrix} c & -s & 0 \\ s & c & 0 \\ 0 & 0 & 1 \end{bmatrix}, \tag{15}
$$

where $c^2 + s^2 = 1$, hence the sought homography is given by $H \sim R_z + tn^T$, where $t = [t_x, t_y, 0]^T$ is a translation vector and $n = [0, 0, 1]^T$ is a floor normal. Let us consider the modified DLT equations (3) again, but this time using two point correspondences. Using the first and third rows, we note that there are in total five unknowns—c, s, t_x, t_y and the radial distortion parameter λ—and in total eleven monomials, hence we may write the system as $Mv = 0$, where M is a 4×11 matrix and v is the vector of monomials. Furthermore, of these eleven monomials, we find only four which contain the variables c and s. Therefore, it is possible to use Gauss–Jordan elimination to eliminate these variables. The corresponding system, after elimination, is on the form

$$\hat{M} = \begin{matrix} \lambda c \ \ c \ \ \lambda s \ \ s \ \ \lambda t_x \ \ t_x \ \ \lambda^2 t_y \ \ \lambda t_y \ \ t_y \ \ \lambda \ \ 1 \\ \begin{bmatrix} 1 & & & & \bullet & \bullet & \bullet & \bullet & \bullet & \bullet & \bullet \\ & 1 & & & \bullet & \bullet & 0 & \bullet & \bullet & 0 & 0 \\ & & 1 & & \bullet & \bullet & \bullet & \bullet & \bullet & \bullet & \bullet \\ & & & 1 & \bullet & \bullet & 0 & \bullet & \bullet & 0 & 0 \end{bmatrix} \end{matrix}. \tag{16}$$

Notice the pattern of zeros emerging in the eliminated system. This, and other more intricate relations, between the coefficients are necessary to account for in order to create an accurate polynomial solver.

From the above system we may introduce the functions g_i, such that

$$\begin{aligned} \lambda c + g_1(t_x, t_y, \lambda) &= 0, \\ c + g_2(t_x, t_y, \lambda) &= 0, \\ \lambda s + g_3(t_x, t_y, \lambda) &= 0, \\ s + g_4(t_x, t_y, \lambda) &= 0 . \end{aligned} \tag{17}$$

where $g_i(t_x, t_y, \lambda)$ are polynomials in the variables t_x, t_y and λ. Furthermore, we utilize the two relations

$$\begin{aligned} g_1(t_x, t_y, \lambda) &= \lambda g_2(t_x, t_y, \lambda), \\ g_3(t_x, t_y, \lambda) &= \lambda g_4(t_x, t_y, \lambda) . \end{aligned} \tag{18}$$

The constraint $c^2 + s^2 = 1$ translates into

$$g_2^2(t_x, t_y, \lambda) + g_4^2(t_x, t_y, \lambda) = 1 . \tag{19}$$

Now, we have a reduced system with three unknowns—t_x, t_y and λ—given by (18) and (19). It turns out that (18) are cubic and (19) are quartic, and by analyzing the dimension of the corresponding quotient ring, we find that the system has six solutions in total (it can be verified that the original system has six solutions as well). Using [15] an elimination template of size 18×24 was constructed.

5   Experiments

5.1   Synthetic Data

In this section we investigate the numerical stability and noise sensitivity of the proposed solver. We generate synthetic homographies, compatible with the

general planar motion model (with and without tilt), as well as distortion parameters. Random scene points are generated using the homography and subsequently distorted using the division model.

The polynomial solvers were generated according to Sect. 4 in C++, and the
mean runtime for the 4 point solver is 730 μs and for the 2 point solver 13 μs
(measured over 100,000 instances on a standard desktop computer).

5.2 Numerical Stability

By using the described method, we generate noise-free problem instances. Similarly to [11], we use physically reasonable parameters, and cover a wide range
of distortions by allowing the distortion parameter λ to be chosen at random in
the interval $[-0.7, 0]$. In Fig. 2 we show the error histogram for 100,000 random
problem instances. When measuring the Frobenius norm error, the homographies
have been normalized to $h_{33} = 1$.

Input   **Output**

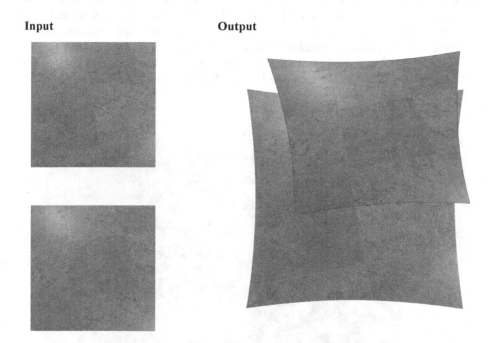

Fig. 5. Two radially distorted images (left) and the rectified and stitched panorama.
The distortion parameter and homography was obtained using the proposed solver
in a RANSAC framework. Blue border added for visualization. Figure and caption
reproduced from [25]. (Color figure online)

From the histogram of the four point solver, we conclude that most parameters are estimated accurately, with an error in the range of 10^{-10}. Such
an error is acceptable for most applications; however, some errors are higher,

reaching an error around 10^{-2}. After careful analysis, we attribute this to the ten degree polynomial, which was added to conform with one of the original quartic constraints necessary for making the proposed solver compatible with the general planar motion model. Luckily, errors of the higher magnitude is less frequently occurring, and can be efficiently discarded in a robust framework, such as RANSAC. We will show that this is the case in the coming sections.

For the two point solver the errors are negligible for most computer vision applications, and is also a strong candidate for a robust framework, given that the assumptions of known tilt are met.

5.3 Noise Sensitivity

Similar to the previous section we generate synthetic problem instances, but corrupt the radially distorted image coordinates with Gaussian noise with a variance σ^2. The noise is varied from mild to severe and at every noise level 10,000 problem instances were generated and the corresponding error measured. As a comparison, the five point method based on the QEP approach [5] was used.

The result is shown in Fig. 3. Note that the mean error for both quantities are lower for the proposed method compared to the five point method, for all noise levels. Analogously, but with known overhead tilt, we compare the two point solver to the other methods, see Fig. 4. Here we see a clear benefit over the other, more general, methods.

Fig. 6. Setup used in the panorama stitching experiment. Figure and caption reproduced from [25].

5.4   Image Stitching

In this section, we use the proposed four point solver in a classic stitching pipeline based on a standard approach for estimating a homography. The pipeline consists of first detecting and extracting SURF keypoints, followed by nearest neighbor matching. From all matched keypoints we select four at random and feed to the proposed solver in a RANSAC framework. The input images are taken using a digital camera with a fish-eye lens mounted on a tripod, overlooking a textured floor, see Fig. 6. The camera tilt was fixed during the experiment, and only the tripod itself was moved, hence generating a motion compatible with the general planar motion model.

The output from the experiment is shown in Fig. 5. Bundle adjustment or other non-linear refinements of the obtained homography was not performed. Apart from being aligned with the correct edges we also note that lines that are straight in reality also appear straight in the final panorama, thus indicating that the radial distortion parameter was correctly estimated.

In terms of the efficiency of the robust framework, we use the same input images and compare the five point solver [5] with the proposed solver. This is done by recording the number of inliers as a function of the number of RANSAC iterations. We repeat the experiment 500 times, and show the average result in Fig. 7, which shows that the proposed method consistently has a higher number of inliers.

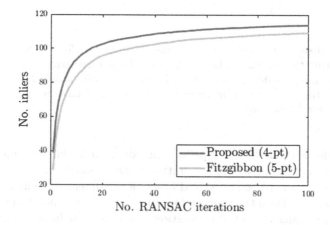

Fig. 7. Number of inliers vs. number of RANSAC iterations for the images in Fig. 5. The data has been averaged over 500 test instances. Figure and caption reproduced from [25].

5.5   Application to Visual Odometry

In this section we use real data from a mobile robot of model Fraunhofer IPA rob@work. The sequence was originally used in [28], but the radial distortion profile was pre-calibrated. On the mobile robot a camera is mounted rigidly, with an unknown overhead tilt, which excludes the application of the two point solver. The distortion is clearly noticeable and the field of view is almost entirely of the textured floor upon which the robot travels. Furthermore, the robot is equipped with omni-directional wheels, which allows for pure rotations. A reference system with an absolute accuracy of 100 μm tracks the robot as it moves about, and the resulting data is used as ground truth.

We consider three sequences:

Line. Forward motion in a straight line with a constant orientation (320 images),
Turn. Forward motion while rotating, resulting in a slight turn (344 images),
Parallel Parking. Forward motion followed by a sharp turn, while keeping constant rotation (325 images).

Fig. 8. (Left) Histogram of estimated distortion parameters for the proposed method evaluating during the *parallel parking* sequence. The selected parameter λ^* is marked with a dashed line. (Middle) Undistorted image of a calibration chart, not part of the sequence. (Right) Rectified image using the estimated parameter λ^*. Figure and caption reproduced from [25].

We consider a standard VO pipeline, including an initial solution via homography estimation, from which the initial camera poses are estimated (both intrinsic and extrinsic parameters) and finally a non-linear refinement step using bundle adjustment. Both the proposed method and the five point method [5] are capable of producing an initial estimation through inter-image homographies. Given a pair of consecutive images we may estimate the distortion parameter as well as the homography, using either solver, in a RANSAC framework. To extract the full set of motion parameters, we use the method in [27], hence establishing the initial poses. The estimated robot trajectory can then be extracted and compared to the ground truth. Note that in a complete VO pipeline, the initial position is important in order to avoid excessive amounts of bundle adjustment iterations, as these typically become large-scale optimization problems. Therefore, it is of interest to decrease the number of necessary iterations, by supplying a good initial guess.

The methods are comparable in terms of accuracy, as can be seen in Fig. 9, with a slight preference for the proposed method. As noted in [23,24], there is no significant boost in performance by pre-optimizing early on in the VO pipeline. One of the main issues is that the constant overhead tilt, due to the camera being rigidly mounted onto the robot, is not enforced throughout the entire trajectory by only considering a single homography. For consistency, one must consider an entire sequence of homographies. Nevertheless, the proposed method benefits from the same performance gain as was noted in Sect. 5.4; namely, that the number of RANSAC iterations required are fewer than for the five point method.

The problem with considering only a single homography also affects the estimation of the radial distortion coefficient. In return, every pair of consecutive images yields a new estimate; however, we know a priori that it is constant through the trajectory. We propose using histogram voting as a robust way to obtain an initial guess. To evaluate the performance we use previously unseen images of calibration charts, that were acquired during the creation of the robot test sequences. We proceed by considering the *parallel parking* test sequence, and use the estimated parameters as a basis for the histogram voting experiment, see Fig. 8. As can be seen, the chosen parameter λ^*, yields an acceptable initial solution, to be refined in a bundle adjustment framework.

5.6   Application to Aerial Imagery

In this final section we test the novel two point solver for aerial imagery. We use the TNT Aerial VideoTestset (TAVT) [19]. In this dataset, video sequences from a UAV have been recorded, at varying flight heights. The onboard global shutter camera is recording in full HDTV resolution at 30 fps, and suffers from mild radial distortion. Although the distortion is not severe, it was shown in [18] that failure to compensate for it results in severely distorted mosaicing attempts.

We use the sequences recorded at higher altitudes, in this case 1000 m and 1500 m above ground, as these are not affected as much by potential non-zero and non-constant tilt, making the two point solver suitable. The solver is incorporated in a RANSAC framework, and the pipeline is identical to previous setups for real images. The sequences are subsampled to include every tenth image of the original sequences, hence contain 117 and 158 images each. The resulting mosaics are shown in Fig. 10. Note that no non-linear optimization has been performed, nor histogram voting to determine the distortion profile. Yet, even for this simple pipeline, we manage to produce visually acceptable results, similar to those of the original articles [18,19]. Perhaps the only noticeable difference is the lack of blending, seam-finding and other processing involved; however, these artifacts do not stem from the solver.

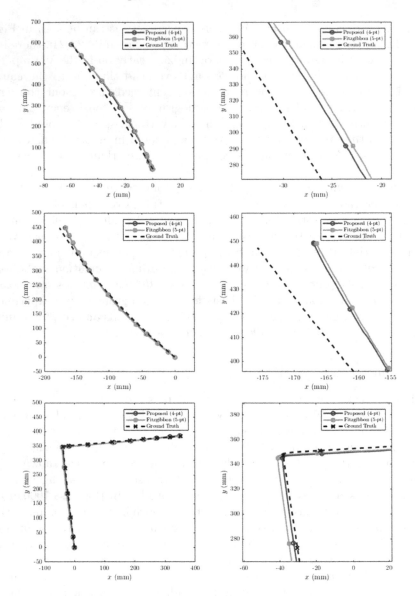

Fig. 9. Estimated trajectories for *line*, *turn* and *parallel parking* of the VO experiment in Sect. 5.5. Images to the left show the entire trajectory, and the ones to the right are zoomed in on a region of interest. Figure and caption reproduced from [25].

Fig. 10. Mosaics from the 1000 m sequence (top) and 1500 m sequence of the TAVT dataset [19] obtained using the proposed two point solver.

6 Conclusions

In this paper, we studied simultaneous radial distortion correction and motion estimation for planar motion. We proposed two polynomial solvers for estimating the homography and distortion parameter, and showed that they are sufficiently numerically robust and fast to be incorporated in a real-time VO pipeline. The proposed solvers were tested rigorously on both synthetic and real data, and were shown to be on par or superior to competing methods.

References

1. Bhayani, S., Kukelova, Z., Heikkila, J.: A sparse resultant based method for efficient minimal solvers. In: Computer Vision and Pattern Recognition (CVPR), June 2020
2. Brown, D.C.: Decentering distortion of lenses. Photogram. Eng. **32**, 444–462 (1966)
3. Chen, T., Liu, Y.H.: A robust approach for structure from planar motion by stereo image sequences. Mach. Vis. Appl. (MVA) **17**(3), 197–209 (2006)
4. Cox, D.A., Little, J., O'Shea, D.: Using Algebraic Geometry. Graduate Texts in Mathematics. Springer, New York (2005)
5. Fitzgibbon, A.W.: Simultaneous linear estimation of multiple view geometry and lens distortion. In: Conference on Computer Vision and Pattern Recognition (CVPR), December 2001
6. Hajjdiab, H., Laganière, R.: Vision-based multi-robot simultaneous localization and mapping. In: Canadian Conference on Computer and Robot Vision (CRV), London, ON, Canada, pp. 155–162, May 2004
7. Hartley, R.I., Zisserman, A.: Multiple View Geometry in Computer Vision, 2nd edn. Cambridge University Press, Cambridge (2004)

8. Kayumbi, G., Cavallaro, A.: Multiview trajectory mapping using homography with lens distortion correction. EURASIP J. Image Video Process. **2008**(1), 1–11 (2008). https://doi.org/10.1155/2008/145715
9. Kukelova, Z., Bujnak, M., Pajdla, T.: Automatic generator of minimal problem solvers. In: Forsyth, D., Torr, P., Zisserman, A. (eds.) ECCV 2008. LNCS, vol. 5304, pp. 302–315. Springer, Heidelberg (2008). https://doi.org/10.1007/978-3-540-88690-7_23
10. Kukelova, Z., Bujnak, M., Pajdla, T.: Polynomial eigenvalue solutions to the 5-pt and 6-pt relative pose problems. In: British Machine Vision Conference (BMVC) (2008)
11. Kukelova, Z., Heller, J., Bujnak, M., Pajdla, T.: Radial distortion homography. In: Conference on Computer Vision and Pattern Recognition (CVPR), pp. 639–647, June 2015
12. Larsson, V., Åström, K.: Uncovering symmetries in polynomial systems. In: Leibe, B., Matas, J., Sebe, N., Welling, M. (eds.) ECCV 2016. LNCS, vol. 9907, pp. 252–267. Springer, Cham (2016). https://doi.org/10.1007/978-3-319-46487-9_16
13. Larsson, V., Åström, K., Oskarsson, M.: Efficient solvers for minimal problems by syzygy-based reduction. In: Computer Vision and Pattern Recognition (CVPR), pp. 2383–2392, July 2017
14. Larsson, V., Åström, K., Oskarsson, M.: Polynomial solvers for saturated ideals. In: International Conference on Computer Vision (ICCV), pp. 2307–2316, October 2017
15. Larsson, V., Kukelova, Z., Zheng, Y.: Camera pose estimation with unknown principal point. In: Computer Vision and Pattern Recognition (CVPR), pp. 2984–2992 (2018)
16. Larsson, V., Oskarsson, M., Åström, K., Wallis, A., Kukelova, Z., Pajdla, T.: Beyond gröbner bases: Basis selection for minimal solvers. In: Computer Vision and Pattern Recognition (CVPR), pp. 3945–3954 (2018)
17. Liang, B., Pears, N.: Visual navigation using planar homographies. In: International Conference on Robotics and Automation (ICRA), Washington, DC, USA, pp. 205–210, May 2002
18. Meuel, H., Ferenz, S., Munderloh, M., Ackermann, H., Ostermann, J.: In-loop radial distortion compensation for long-term mosaicking of aerial videos. In: Proceedings of the 23rd IEEE International Conference on Image Processing (ICIP), pp. 2961–2965, September 2016
19. Meuel, H., Munderloh, M., Reso, M., Ostermann, J.: Mesh-based piecewise planar motion compensation and optical flow clustering for ROI coding. APSIPA Trans. Sign. Inf. Process. **4**, e13 (2015)
20. Ortín, D., Montiel, J.M.M.: Indoor robot motion based on monocular images. Robotica **19**(3), 331–342 (2001)
21. Pritts, J., Kukelova, Z., Larsson, V., Chum, O.: Radially-distorted conjugate translations. In: Conference on Computer Vision and Pattern Recognition (CVPR) (2018)
22. Pritts, J., Kukelova, Z., Larsson, V., Chum, O.: Rectification from radially-distorted scales. In: Jawahar, C.V., Li, H., Mori, G., Schindler, K. (eds.) ACCV 2018. LNCS, vol. 11365, pp. 36–52. Springer, Cham (2019). https://doi.org/10.1007/978-3-030-20873-8_3
23. Valtonen Örnhag, M., Wadenbäck, M.: Enforcing the general planar motion model: bundle adjustment for planar scenes. In: De Marsico, M., Sanniti di Baja, G., Fred, A. (eds.) ICPRAM 2019. LNCS, vol. 11996, pp. 119–135. Springer, Cham (2020). https://doi.org/10.1007/978-3-030-40014-9_6

24. Valtonen Örnhag, M.: Fast non-minimal solvers for planar motion compatible homographies. In: International Conference on Pattern Recognition Applications and Methods (ICPRAM), Prague, Czech Republic, pp. 40–51, February 2019
25. Valtonen Örnhag, M.: Radially distorted planar motion compatible homographies. In: International Conference on Pattern Recognition Applications and Methods (ICPRAM), pp. 280–288 (2020)
26. Wadenbäck, M., Heyden, A.: Planar motion and hand-eye calibration using inter-image homographies from a planar scene. In: International Conference on Computer Vision Theory and Applications (VISAPP), pp. 164–168 (2013)
27. Wadenbäck, M., Heyden, A.: Ego-motion recovery and robust tilt estimation for planar motion using several homographies. In: International Conference on Computer Vision Theory and Applications (VISAPP), pp. 635–639, January 2014
28. Wadenbäck, M., Karlsson, M., Heyden, A., Robertsson, A., Johansson, R.: Visual odometry from two point correspondences and initial automatic tilt calibration. In: International Joint Conference on Computer Vision, Imaging and Computer Graphics Theory and Applications (VISIGRAPP 2017), pp. 340–346 (2017)
29. Wadenbäck, M., Åström, K., Heyden, A.: Recovering planar motion from homographies obtained using a 2.5-point solver for a polynomial system. In: International Conference on Image Processing (ICIP), pp. 2966–2970 (2016)
30. Zienkiewicz, J., Davison, A.J.: Extrinsics autocalibration for dense planar visual odometry. J. Field Robot. (JFR) **32**(5), 803–825 (2015)

A Preliminary Study on Tree-Top Detection and Deep Learning Classification Using Drone Image Mosaics of Japanese Mixed Forests

Yago Diez[1]([✉])[iD], Sarah Kentsch[2][iD], Maximo Larry Lopez Caceres[2][iD],
Koma Moritake[1], Ha Trang Nguyen[2], Daniel Serrano[3], and Ferran Roure[3][iD]

[1] Faculty of Science, Yamagata University, Yamagata, Japan
yagodiezdonoso@gmail.com, yago@sci.kj.yamagata-u.ac.jp
[2] Faculty of Agriculture, Yamagata University, Yamagata, Japan
[3] Eurecat, Centre Tecnològic de Catalunya, Barcelona, Spain

Abstract. Tree counting and classification tasks in forestry are often addressed by costly, in terms of labour and money, field surveys carried on manually by forestry experts. Consequently, computer vision techniques have been used to automatically detect tree tops and classify them in terms of species or plant health status. The success of the algorithms are highly dependent on the data, and most significantly in its quantity and in the number of challenges it presents. In this work we used Unmanned Aerial Vehicles to acquired extremely challenging data from natural Japanese mixed forests. In a first step, six common clustering algorithms were used for tree top detection. Furthermore, we also assessed the usability of five different deep learning architectures to classify tree tops corresponding to trees in different degrees of affectation from a parasite infestation. Data covering an area of 40 ha are used in extensive experiments resulting in a detection accuracy of over 80% with high location accuracy and up to 90% with lower accuracy. Classification results produced by our algorithms reached error rates as low as 0.096 for classification. Data acquisition and runtime considerations show that this techniques is useful to process real forest data.

Keywords: Computer vision · Tree detection · Tree classification · Mixed forests · Clustering techniques

1 Introduction and State of the Art

The average global forest cover around 30% of the surface [4], while forests in Japan occupy approximately 68% of its territory, playing an important role in the ecosystem. A large part of them is made up of deciduous mixed forest [54]. Since the early 20th century, research on these issues is carried out using manual land surveys [18,31,36], which are labor-intensive, expensive and often require high degrees of expertise. Understanding their ecologically complexity, due to varying

© Springer Nature Switzerland AG 2020
M. De Marsico et al. (Eds.): ICPRAM 2020, LNCS 12594, pp. 64–86, 2020.
https://doi.org/10.1007/978-3-030-66125-0_5

tree species distribution as well as the interactions between species, is necessary to design adequate management policies [22]. This is specially important in times where climate change creates stress to these ecosystems [4]. The development of methods to gather and process forest information which is fast, efficient and reliable to be able to monitor forests accurately [3].

Unmanned Aerial Vehicles (UAVs) are rapidly becoming an essential tool in forestry applications [19,41–43]. UAVs are remote easy-to-use and inexpensive and acquire are high-resolution images in the range of cm/pixel. This results in highly detailed image information which can be easily accessed and processed automatically [5]. Computer vision techniques are common in a variety of areas ranging from 3D reconstruction [51] to medical imaging [20]. The expansion in several research fields and therewith an increase in data availability started with the appearance of new techniques such as Deep Learning where some well established computer vision concepts such as segmentation, registration or classification are applied [14,42]. The variety of computer vision algorithms techniques used with high-resolution images obtained by drones, allows to use choose algorithms which can be applied for the problem of detecting individual trees.

In the fields of agriculture and forests plantations, accurate information about plant numbers within stands were acquired by manual tree counting [30,37,40,47,52]. In natural forests, detecting individual trees is a necessary task for evaluating the distribution, measuring tree heights or estimating carbon stocks [41,42,58] and tasks in forest management like getting surveys [29,33,49]. However, characteristics of individual trees like their size or the species compositions are challenging in terms of image analysis algorithms [26]. Equally, soil signals and man-made objects may cause decreases of classification accuracy achieved [32,52]. Most of the existing studies are carried out in plantations, since trees are more equally in size and age (often same species) and disturbing factors are reduced, which increases classification accuracy [10,40,53].

In this paper the work presented in [13] was continued by adapting well known clustering and extreme detection computer vision algorithms to locate tree tops in dense and unmanned forests. A new pre-processing step based on filtering the floor section of the data is presented. This new algorithm is included in the pipeline and compared to the previous approach. We have also widened the scope of our study by adding an image classification step that uses deep learning. We classify images corresponding to the tree tops using several deep learning architectures in order to assess the possibility of using these architectures for species or health status classification of trees with the amount of data commonly available in forestry applications. A comprehensive work of the studied algorithms are presented with analysis the correctness, precision and needed time of each strategy. In order to better situate the work in the proper context we have also significantly expanded the discussion on previous work.

The paper is organised as follows. The rest of this section introduces previous studies in the field of tree detection and counting by the use of computer vision. Section 2 describes the tackled problem information about the data acquisition process. An extensive explanation on the data characteristics and the effects on this study are given. Section 3 provide information on the algorithms, pre- and post-processing steps that were performed to overcome data difficulties to detect tree tops. Section 4 provides quantitative evaluation of the results obtained. Finally, the conclusions and considerations on future work in Sect. 5.

1.1 State of Art

In a time of changing climate, natural forests become of great interest to study the effects of climate on tree distribution or forest health [4,8,9]. Tree counting provides useful information for forest (specially plantation) management [2,40,50,53,61]. Single trees detection using automatic methods and image analysis is a challenging problem affected by factors such as tree age and height, tree stand composition, the terrain the forest is set on and lighting conditions at the time of acquisition [26]. Initial studies used tree tops higher intensity values in comparison to the surrounding pixels [21,45,46,48]. Other methods refined an initial set of tree tops [30] using local elevation extrema or classical image segmentation techniques such as Watersheds, Region Growing, or morphological operators. For example, [15] detected points with high grey values and compared performances of Region Growing, Template matching and Brownian motion methods to refine the segmentation and obtain tree crowns. [26] uses a Digital Elevation Model (DEM) to detect seed regions of single trees based on pixel-wise elevation values. [35] made the importance of data evident by comparing different algorithms on different datasets and forest conditions.

Recent studies have been using deep learning approaches to analyze images with higher resolution [10,37,40,61]. For example [37] used a deep learning model to detect and count oil palm trees in satellite images. First, a binary classifier was used to separate the data into tree and background. Then, a sliding window technique was used to refine the segmentation obtaining an accuracy of 96%. On another study, [40] the related problem of separating young and mature oil palm trees was solved with 95% accuracy using two separate deep convolutional neural networks. [12] detect trees and estimate their phisical properties using DEM information. [57] presented a DSM-based floor elimination step and subsequently compared different image modalities (RGB and multispectral) to segment and classify olive trees in a plantation. Multispectral images obtained the best accuracy at 97%.

Most of these used data acquired in plantations while much less attention has been devoted so far to mixed natural forests. Taken into account studies such as [35] that show how most algorithms are highly data-dependent existing algorithms are likely to fail to produce optimal results in challenging environments such as natural mixed forests. The main reason for this is that forests are markedly heterogeneous environments and that the images acquired in them are affected by shadowing and lighting changes. Furthermore, forest composition and, most specially the overlapping of tree crowns, make tree detection a challenging task. Specific examples of how frequent problems in natural forest affect existing methods are: The sensitiveness of region growing to reflectance changes pointed in [30], the difficulties on maximum filtering when dealing with small and young trees as well as problems with template matching in crowded stands (both pointed in [37]). Hence, in this paper we set out to detect tree tops using RGB mosaics and DEMs in an exceedingly challenging scenario due to our forests being natural, unmanaged, mixed and set in areas with steep slopes.

2 Data Gathering, Annotation and Preprocessing

Japanese natural mixed forests are often located in mountainous areas. Our chosen study sites, located in the northern most area of the Asahi mountains and Zao mountain, are representative forests of those areas. In general the studied forests are characterized by steep slopes ranging between 33 and 40% [39], dense structures and high under-story vegetation, which hampers field studies and analysis in forests. For these forests dominate tree species were identified, but accurate information about the distribution of all appearing tree species, their number and location within the forest, as well as their development are not known.

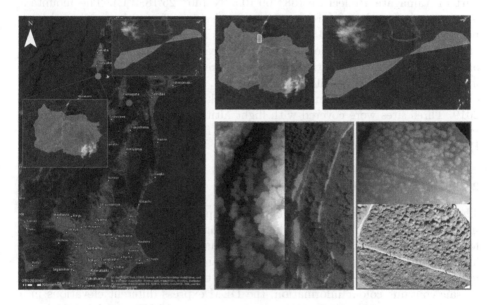

Fig. 1. Shows the location of the study sites (left) and two representative example sites used to detect treetops, DEMs and mosaics (bottom right).

2.1 Data Acquisition

The small user-friendly drones, namely a DJI Phantom 4 and DJI Mavic 2 Pro were used to acquire the data. The drones were used to collect images of the mixed forest and to cover different sites within the forest. The drones took high resolution RGB images, since the Phantom 4 is equipped with 12 megapixel and the Maivc with a 20 megapixel camera. GPS and GLONASS satellite systems are used to georeferenced the position of the drone. A standardize flight protocol was used to assure constant overlaps and flight altitudes during image acquisitions by using the app DJI GS Pro. The pre-programmed flight time was set between 15 min and 30 min considering the area covered per site.

Locations. The diversity of Japanese forests leaded to a selection of different forest environments which represent those special environments (see Fig. 1). One location was chosen in the Yamagata University Research Forest (YURF) located in the northwest of the main island of Japan, Honshu (38° 49'14''N, 139° 47'47''E). As part of the Asahi mountain the 753,02 ha large area represent natural mixed forests. For image collection seven different sites (four river and 3 slope sites) where chosen to represent the characteristics the forest. In the summer season 2019, data gathering was performed in those areas covering 3 to 6 ha per site. Parameters for the flights were set between 80 and 140 m depending on the elevation of the mountain together with an overlap 90 and 96%. Per flight raw images between 214 and 418 were collected.

The second study site is the Zao mountain, a volcano in the southeastern part of Yamagata Prefecture (38° 09'10.5''N 140° 25'18.4''E). The mountain is mostly composed of fir trees (*Abies sachalensis*) affected by moth and bark beetle infestations since 2014. The study sites are located at different altitudes of the mountain. The sites located in lower areas are characterized by a mixture of fir trees with deciduous trees, while the forest develops to a monoculture of fir trees with increasing altitude. Furthermore, with higher altitude the number of infected trees increase. Image collection took place during the summer season 2019. Three sites were covered with flight altitudes between 60 and 70 m, 90% front and side overlap and cover area of each flight ranging between 1 to 2 ha. Per site up to 495 raw images were collected.

2.2 Data Processing and Annotation

The raw images were processed by Metashape software [1]. Metashape used image information and GPS coordinates to align raw images which were transformed into a dense point cloud. The dense cloud is used to create image mosaics and Digital Elevation Models (DEM), which are used in this approach. The differences between the mosaic and the DEM are the stored information. While the mosaic contains colour information, the DEM express different elevations in a gray-scale format. Examples of the mosaics can be seen in Fig. 1 (right) while the center part of the same figure contains examples of DEMs. In total, a number of 10 mosaics, as well as their DEMs were considered for this study. The DEM can be exported as GeoTIFF file from Metashape software in which location information are embedded. Those files cannot be opened in image visualisation software. Therefore, a pre-processing step was done to transform the GeoTIFF into a JPEG file using ArcGIS.

Figure 2 depicts the workflow for pre-processing the data for using them with deep learning techniques. Images were collected and processed in Metashape. Before the annotation process the DEM needed to be converted, and both the DEM and the mosaic were used in GIMP to prepare the annotation for handing them to the algorithms.

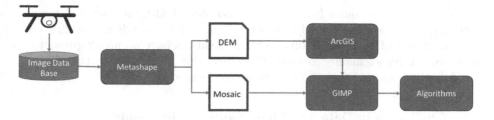

Fig. 2. Overview of the software used to pre-process the data.

The following step was the manually annotation process, done with GIMP, an image manipulation software. The mosaic and the DEM were used as single layers and a third layer was added for the annotations. The annotation process was done by marking higher points in the third layer on basis of the DEM information. The mosaic was used for confirmation that the marked points belongs to tree tops, since the mosaics contained further features, like a rope way. Figure 3 presents a part of one of the mosaics with superimposed annotation data. Besides that, trees on Zao mountain sites were annotated into four categories healthy fir, sick

Fig. 3. Detail of the mosaic data (left), the mosaics (center) and the results of annotation (right), tree tops are presented as white points. This figure originally appeared in the initial version of this work [13].

fir, dead fir and deciduous based on orthomosaics. Healthy firs account for firs with majority branches covered by green leaves. Sick firs are defined as firs with more than half of branches defoliated while dead firs have no needle present on all branches. As we mainly focus on the infestation of fir trees on this site, all deciduous species we simply marked them as deciduous.

2.3 Challenges in Data and Limitations of This Study

Previous studies already used image analysis and computer vision techniques to count trees, especially in agricultural fields. In agricultural fields the trees are planted which has several benefits for computer vision detection algorithms, like thresholding and contour detection. Trees are planted in lines and separated from each other, which makes it easy to differentiate between single trees and soils. The accuracy for tree detection has therefore a high accuracy [23,40,56]. Detecting trees is challenging in well-managed forests, while unmanaged and dense forests, like the Japanese mixed natural forests makes tree detection more difficult. The characteristic of mixed natural forests are overlapping canopies and high density of understory vegetation, which increase the difficulty to differentiate between canopies and bushes. Separation of tree crowns from different tree species is difficult, while it is impossible for the trees of the same species. Tree counting tasks are therefore difficult to conduct. The DEM and its height information offers the possibility to reconstruct forests as a 3D version, which can be a useful tool for detecting trees. The localisation of highest points in regions of interest can help to identify single trees. However, there are few studies done in dense forests with variable tree distributions and their influence on detecting single tree [17,35,60].

The heterogeneity of the forests which we faced complicated the work and the effectiveness of using computer vision techniques. The forests show areas, where a few trees are isolated, while next to it a high number of trees covered the area. Furthermore, the chosen sites show different characteristics in the elevation. As mentioned in Sect. 2.1 there are sites which are located close to the river or on slopes, which has a high impact on the density of the forest, the resolution and the height information of pixels in the mosaics. As lighter pixels represent higher altitudes" the pixel value is always a mix of the altitude and the elevation of the ground. This causes difficulties, when small bushes cover slope areas and pixel information show high values due to the elevation (Fig. 4 top right). Therefore, only regions with trees needed to be detected by the algorithm considering a local maxima. Additionally, the sick trees which can be found in Zao mountain further influence the detection possibility since dead trees are barley represented in DEM. Artifacts at the corners of mosaic appearing due to missing images caused distortion, as well as man-made objects like buildings (Fig. 4 bottom) or electricity towers (Fig. 4 center right) can cause problems with the algorithm. Since the data itself show a high degree of heterogeneity, the used mosaics were divided into classes which represent more homogenous characteristics of the forests in the mosaic. Two mosaics were classified by their high density and their location

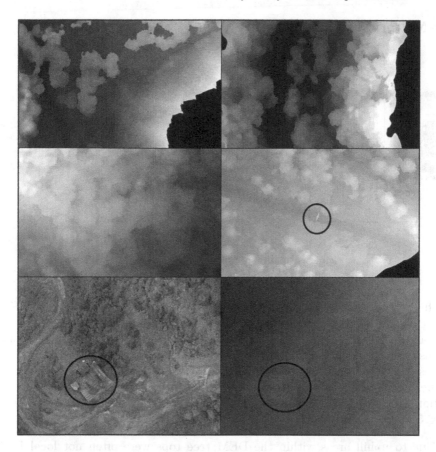

Fig. 4. Data difficulties. The top left image shows a DEM representing a slope with bushes. The top right and center left images represent varying canopy densities in DEMs. The images in the center right and bottom, show the mosaic and the DEM of the same area containing distortion caused by man-made objects. This figure originally appeared in the initial version of this work [13].

in steep slopes. A certain degree of tree density variability can be compensated with the algorithms used. However, the other mosaics represent characteristics highly different from those two DEMs and good results could not be obtained by a single set of parameters, they were discarded. The results presented were obtained by using the remaining 8 mosaics.

3   Materials and Methods

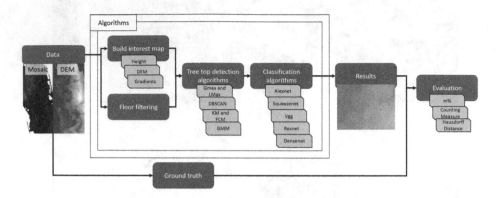

Fig. 5. Pipeline of the studied algorithms.

In this section we present the algorithms used to extract tree tops from DEMs and classify the trees represented by those tree tops. Taking previous works into account (see, for example, [41]) our initial aim was to search for local pixel intensity maxima in the DEM. However, the data presented additional challenges, which increased numbers of tree candidate points outside of the regions properly containing trees. This happened due to the Orography of our data collection sites (see Sect. 2.3). Two examples of the problems encountered are that (Fig. 5):

- Due to uphill areas within the DEM tree tops were often not local DEM maxima
- There were regions without trees at different altitude values (sometimes including the DEM global maximum).

Tree densities in different DEMs, as well as within one DEM show significant variations as three windows with the same size contained no, 2, 4 or 10 tree tops, for example. Tree detection algorithms cannot be used with the same set of parameters for the whole of each mosaic.

As a result, a first step in our algorithm aimed at finding the "interest regions" containing trees or filtering out the contained floor. Section 3.1 presents two algorithms to achieve this goal. After the regions were determined to actually contain trees then we run several well-known clustering algorithms in order to extract tree tops (Sect. 3.2). Finally, small regions around the tree tops where used with several Deep Learning Classifier architectures in Sect. 3.3.

3.1   Interest Region Extraction

Interest Maps Using DEM Values, and Gradients. The strategy followed the three steps described by [13]. First, the DEM was divided in interest regions according to heights associated to each pixel by a thresholding algorithm. A value of 0 was assigned to the floor, which were not located in slope areas and then discarded. High value pixel were assigned a 2 representing tree tops, which were not received in all mosaics. Pixels which could not clearly identified as part of the previous mentioned values got a value of 1. In the second step of the algorithm the presence or absence of high DEM intensity gradients were used to divide regions. The Sobel filter [11] identified large gradients in x and y directions, which were added into a single gradient image to assigned regions without a gradient a value of 0, the ones with a value of 2. A morphological closing operator [24] was further used to find tree tops in enclosed regions of the tree crowns. A combination of the described labels result into:

- 0 → Pixel assigned to the floor without elevations.
- 1 → Pixels which do not belong to floor or high pixel values and with no gradients.
- 2 → Pixels with a high value and no gradients.
- 3 → Pixels not belonging to floor nor being high, but with Gradients present.
- 4 → High pixel with gradients.

Figure 6 shows an example of an interest map. The detailed subfigure shows that higher tree top densities are marked with brighter pixel intensities representing higher interest. Difficulties of the terrain can be seen in the bottom left corner of the main figure, where sections of high interest contain no trees, but bushes in an uphill part having pixel values close to the ones of tree tops.

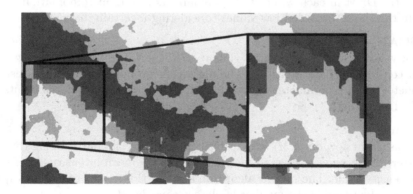

Fig. 6. Example of an interest map with superimposed tree tops marked as points. This figure originally appeared in the initial version of this work [13].

Floor Filtering. In this second strategy to filter out the floor of the DEM, information from the mosaics were incorporated. Specifically, three different strategies we used. 1) As shadows are known to belong to the floor regions, the mosaic was turned into grayscale representation and blurring and thresholding was used to detect darker areas (corresponding to shadows). 2) Color parameters were considered and thresholding used to filter out all areas with low green values including dirt sections or river areas as can be seen in Fig. 1. 3) Finally lower pixels in the DEM were filtered out. The result from these strategies was a binary mask representing the regions belonging to the floor (black) or to trees (white). This mask was extended using several iterations of a sliding window strategy by painting pixels within a given altitude threshold of floor pixels. Thus, slope regions were identify that ascended slowly without sudden changes in altitude by the presence of trees. The resulting floor binary mask was then used to mask out the part of the DEM containing the floor.

3.2   Tree Top Detection Algorithm

Several algorithms were applied on the masks where regions without trees were filtered out. A sliding window technique was applied, using different window sizes which affects the performance of the algorithms. One of the six tree top detection algorithms run for each position of the window. Since the studied algorithms are presented in [13] the following description is kept short, for detailed information refer to the aforementioned reference.

Iterative Global Maxima
The iterative Global Maxima (GMax) is a simple and fast algorithm consists on finding the maximum intensity value in each window.

Peak Local Maxima
This algorithm (from now on as *LMax*) identified several local maxima presented within the DEM in each window. A gaussian smoothing in combination with a certain threshold discarded low values considering a certain distance.

DBSCAN
"Density based spatial clustering" (short *DBSCAN*) [16] is a clustering algorithm considering data densities. The algorithm groups nearby points using a parameter ϵ and a parameter ms to filter cluster centers, then marks points not grouped as outliers.

K-Means
K-Means (from now om *KM*) is a clustering algorithm [38] partitioning the data k clusters. Each pixel belongs to the cluster with the mean intensity closer to its own intensity value. The specific algorithm used for this as well as the subsequent clustering algorithm is the number of classes considered nc.

Fuzzy C-Means
As a variation of K-Means, Fuzzy C-Means (*FCM*) algorithm assigns each pixel a probability to belong to each existing cluster [6]. Computed centroids depending on the probability of each pixel to belong to a class and a fuzziness parameter changing weight of the contribution of each pixel are considered.

Gaussian Mixture Model
The Gaussian Mixture Model *GMM* algorithm clusters data considering every cluster as a normal (or Gaussian) random variable. Pixel probabilities are computed to assign them to clusters (or Gaussians) by defining Gaussian parameters and updated under the use of an expectation maximization algorithm. The algorithm ends when a certain convergence criterion is held.

Use of Interest Maps to Refine the Detected Tree Tops. For all algorithms, any tree top detected in the section identified as not containing trees, was discarded. For all of the other sections, tree tops were assigned an "uncertainty" region in the shape of a disk of varying radius. Then intersecting uncertainty reasons were merged and a single representative tree top was used. The interest map was used to make the uncertainty regions in lower interest regions have larger radii. With this, the number of points in lower interest regions was reduced.

For the three parameterised clustering algorithms (KM, FCM, GMM), the average of the interest map labels of the pixels in each window was used to adjust the number of clusters being detected with higher interest regions being assigned more clusters.

3.3   Tree Top Classification

Tree top classification is a central step in many forestry applications such as labeling the trees in a mosaic according to their species or determining the health status of trees (as infestations as happens in one of our data acquisition locations). In order to capture the distinctive characteristics of each tree type, a small square patch around each tree top were sampled (indicated by a single points at its center). Then, each patch was assigned a class according to the manual annotation codifying the classes that could be found in the image as mentioned in Sect. 2.1 (Healthy Fir, Sick Fir, Dead Fir and deciduous). Using this information, the problem was formalised in terms of deep learning as a classical single-label classification problem using the patches extracted around the tree tops. This problem was solved using one of the following deep learning classifiers:

1. Alexnet [34] is one of the first widely used convolutional neural networks, composed of eight layers (five convolutional layers sometimes followed by max-pooling layers) and three fully connected layers).
2. Squeezenet [28] used so-called squeeze filters, including point-wise filter to reduce the number of parameters needed. A similar accuracy to Alexnet was claimed with fewer parameters.
3. Vgg [55] represents an evolution of the Alexnet network that allowed for an increased number of layers (16 in the version considered in our work) by using smaller convolutional filters.
4. Resnet [25] was one of the first DL architectures to allow higher number of layers by including blocks composed of convolution, batch normalization and ReLU. In the current work its version with 50 layers had been used.

5. Densenet [27] use a larger number of connections between layers to claim increased parameter efficiency and better feature propagation that allows them to work with even more layers (121 in this work).

All these DL classifiers were initialised used Imagenet weights. See, for example, [34]. The classifiers where trained using the manually annotated tree points and information of the tree health classes annotated in the mosaic. The data was randomly divided into two subsets of 80% for training and 20% for testing.

4   Experiments

Continuing the work presented in [13], all the algorithms tested in this section were implemented in python [59]. The opencv library [7] was used for low-level image operations and scikit-learn [44] was used to retrieve implementations of clustering algorithms.

4.1   Tree Top Detection

In this section we report the performance of the six methods studied in terms of the same three objective measures presented in [13]. In this case we provide thir formulae with a very succinct description and refer the reader to the mentioned reference for details.

Hausdorff Distance

$$\mathrm{d}_H(A, B) = \max\left\{ \sup_{a \in A} \inf_{b \in B} \mathrm{d}(a, b), \sup_{b \in B} \inf_{a \in A} \mathrm{d}(a, b) \right\}$$

This metric provides a way to measure to measure distances between points but is vulnerable to outlier values and is, thus completed with two more metrics:

Matched Ground Truth Points Percentage ($m\%$)
The percentage of ground truth points matched gives us an indication of what percentage of the tree tops were detected by defining an acceptable uncertainty region as a circle of a fixed radius around each ground truth point. However this measure was vulnerable to methods finding many point which would eventually end up finding points close to all ground truth points but would not coincide with what we intuitively consider a good prediction. To fix this we considered a third metric:

Counting Measure
Stands for the difference of the trees present in the mosaic "n", with the number of tree tops detected "d" weighted over the number of trees $cnt = \frac{n-d}{n}$.

Only methods achieving good results for the three metrics at the same time (as low as possible for Hausdorff and cnt and as close to 100 as possible for $m\%$) are reported.

4.2   Interest Region Extraction

Tables 1, 2 and 3 present quantitative results for this experiment. An example of the data used as well as result for some of the methods can be found in Fig. 7. Tables 1, 2 appeared in [13] and are provided for ease of comparison, a new interest region extraction is summarised in Table 3 and compared to previous results.

Table 1. Comparison 0f pre-processing algorithms.

Hausdorff distance	GMax	LMax	DBSCAN	KM	FCM	GMM
Interest map	1249.96	1456.74	1194.10	1198.85	1258.62	1170.26
Floor filtering	1316.61	1361.42	1210.10	1142.51	1256.22	1109.28

Table 1 presents the average Hausdorff distance, over all 8 mosaics considered, for the six methods studied with the two interest region extraction techniques studied. Best results are obtained by GMM (1170.26/1109.28), DBSCAN (1194.10/1210.10) and KM (1198.85/1142.51). GMax and FCM obtain results close to 1250 while the result of LMax is close to 1400. This indicates a superior performance in terms of this distance of clustering methods over those aimed at finding intensity maxima. The floor filtering approach obtained slightly better results for this criterion for the best performing methods.

Tables 2 and 3 presents results for the cnt and $m\%$ measures for each method and DEM. Table 2 corresponds to the interest map pre-process while Table 3 refers to the floor filtering pre-process. The tables are divided into two parts, the top parts contain information about five of the DEMs while the lower parts contains information on the remaining three as well as the average. Each row corresponds to one method and each pair of columns to the performances of all the studied methods for one particular DEM. The final two columns contain the averages of the cnt and $m\%$ measures. Notice that positive cnt values indicate that the algorithm overestimated the number of trees, negative values indicate underestimation and that the average presented was computed using average values so as not to cancel both errors out.

For the interest map pre-process, (Table 3), best results are observed for the GMax algorithm achieving the best matched point percentage and counting measure (90.64, 8.09). High results of over 80% on matching percentage were obtained by FCM (81.88, 13.15), GMM (81.15, 14.25) AND DBSCAN (80.94, 14.28). KM is able to match slightly fewer tree tops but is better at counting them (76.90, 11.50) while LMax obtains the worst results with still high matched tree percentage but a clear tendency to overestimate the number of trees producing a bad cnt value (72.47, 27.49). Conversely, results presented in Table 3 and referring to the floor filtering pre-process show how best results were observed for the GMax algorithm achieving the best matched point percentage and counting measure (85.68, 9.41). High results of over 80% on matching

Table 2. Tree crown detection method performance with the Interest Map Preprocess. This table originally appeared in the initial version of this work [13].

DEM	1		2		3		4		5	
Method	*m%*	*cnt*	*m%*	*cnt*	*m%*	*cnt*	*m%*	*cnt*	*m%*	*cnt*
GMax	90,34	-15,91	92,93	0,51	91,48	13,77	89,78	3,11	85,83	16,25
LMax	85,23	10,23	78,79	12,12	65,57	30,16	53,33	32,89	82,92	25
DBSCAN	77,84	-21,02	80,81	-3,28	90,16	-15,08	76	-13,33	80,83	4,58
KM	64,2	5,11	72,22	22,73	78,69	0	69,78	10,67	80,42	17,08
FCM	72,73	-5,11	73,74	18,18	83,61	-15,41	77,78	-1,78	84,17	1,67
GMM	70,45	-10,23	72,22	19,44	81,64	-10,49	76,44	-2,67	82,92	5,83
DEM	6		7		8		AVERAGE			
Method	*m%*	*cnt*	*m%*	*cnt*	*m%*	*cnt*	*m%*		*cnt*	
GMax	91,13	0	88,51	13,75	95,15	1,43	90,64		8,09	
LMax	66,01	37,44	77,59	45,2	70,29	26,86	72,47		27,49	
DBSCAN	70,94	-7,88	83,8	11,11	87,14	-38	80,94		14,28	
KM	71,92	3,94	88,51	6,21	89,43	-26,29	76,90		11,50	
FCM	76,35	-9,85	92,09	-12,62	94,57	-40,57	81,88		13,15	
GMM	79,8	-15,27	92,28	-12,62	93,43	-37,43	81,15		14,25	

Table 3. Tree crown detection method performance with the Floor Filtering Preprocess.

DEM	1		2		3		4		5	
Method	*m%*	*cnt*	*m%*	*cnt*	*m%*	*cnt*	*m%*	*cnt*	*m%*	*cnt*
GMax	85.94	7.81	82.86	15.43	89.87	11.39	85.53	7.57	79.92	7.53
LMax	83.85	17.19	72.57	1.71	76.71	5.32	60.20	27.96	78.24	16.32
DBSCAN	64.58	5.21	68.57	12.57	75.44	9.37	80.26	8.22	60.67	16.74
KM	79.17	7.81	77.14	9.71	70.13	5.82	74.67	8.22	87.87	8.37
FCM	80.21	5.21	78.29	24.00	69.87	4.05	75.33	19.08	88.70	13.81
GMM	74.48	17.19	66.29	1.14	58.48	25.32	74.34	6.25	73.64	23.01
DEM	6		7		8		AVERAGE			
Method	*m%*	*cnt*	*m%*	*cnt*	*m%*	*cnt*	*m%*		*cnt*	
GMax	86.63	13.37	84.15	2.45	90.54	9.74	85.68		9.41	
LMax	71.29	6.93	88.11	15.28	83.38	37.54	76.79		16.03	
DBSCAN	69.80	23.76	61.70	12.64	80.80	25.50	70.23		14.25	
KM	83.17	29.21	85.85	7.92	90.54	49.28	81.07		15.79	
FCM	82.67	46.04	87.74	14.53	90.54	59.60	81.67		23.29	
GMM	74.75	6.93	83.96	6.60	81.66	14.61	73.45		12.63	

percentage were obtained by KM (81.07, 15.79) and FCM (81.67, 23.29). This last method, though, is much less precise when counting trees. Other methods obtain satisfactory results with counting errors around 15% and detection rates from 70 to 76%.

As opposed to what was observed for the Hausdorff metric, best results seem to be obtained for this metric for the methods that rely on DEM intensity maxima. Best results overall where obtained by the interest map pre-process and GMax algorithm although most methods performed better with the Floor filtering pre-process.

Table 1 seem to be painting a slightly different picture to Tables 2 and 3 concerning method performance. We believe the main reason for this has to with the behaviour of algorithms in areas of extreme point tree top density. That is, areas with very few or many tree tops. On the one hand, the GMax algorithm tends to place a similar number of points in all these areas (this behaviour is corrected to a certain extent by the use of interest maps detailed in Sect. 3.2). Conversely, algorithms such as GMM and FCM tend to place fewer points than Gmax in lower density areas and more in higher density areas. The extra points in lower density areas heavily penalise the Hausdorff value for GMax while the extra points in high density areas penalise a little bit the counting measure for clustering methods. Figure 7 shows a medium-high density area where GMax has predicted too few points. Moreover, the distance between the predicted points is somewhat large while not large enough so that most of the points are not matched. On the other hand, KM and GMM manage to predict points much closer to the ground truth points but on occasion they also place extra points that detract from their counting score. This seems to agree with the differences in performance obtained by the DEM intensity based methods (most specially GMax) when considered with the two pre-processing algorithms. The floor filtering algorithm results in a more strictly binarised DEM (some areas that appeared as "low priority" but where available in the interest map algorithm become totally unavailable). This results in algorithms that tend to place points further from their true position such as GMax (as expressed by Table 1) not being able to place some of the points at all. Similarly, algorithms that tend to place points closer to their real position benefit from the disappearance of these "low priority" regions resulting in decreased Hausdorff distance with similar (if not improved) counting measure.

4.3   Tree Classification

For this experiment, we considered one of the mosaics from the Zao site presenting Bark Beetle infestation. This site contains Deciduous trees that are not affected by the beetle as well as Evergreen trees of the Fir species. Although in this experiment we focus on this application, the algorithms studied can be used in a wide variety of forestry-related applications. For the current experiment, we annotated each of the pixels of the image as to belong to one of the following classes: Deciduous, Dead Fir, Healthy Fir, Sick Fir. In order to focus on the merits of the classification algorithms, for this experiment we used manually annotated tree tops. A small patch around each tree top (of 100×100 pixels, amounting approximately to a 2 m sided square) was automatically extracted. The position of the corresponding tree top was used along with the manually annotated ground truth on tree health to determine the class the patch belonged to.

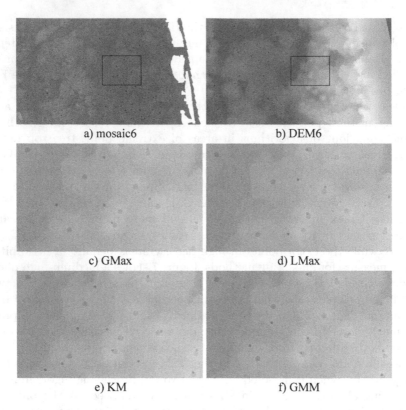

Fig. 7. Example results for selected tree detection algorithms for DEM6. a) The original mosaic image b) contains the corresponding DEM image. In both cases manually annotated ground truth points are marked in black and a section is highlighted. d–e contain results of some of the studied methods superimposed a DEM section. Larger points stand for ground truth points while the smaller ones represent predicted points. This figure originally appeared in the initial version of this work [13].

Transfer Learning and Parameter Tuning. Our data set consisted, thus, of patches that belonged to one of the aforementioned categories. The dataset was then divided into 80% training and 20% validation. All deep learning models where initialised using imagenet weights, so transfer learning from a large, general-purpose dataset was performed. As we were using a relatively small number of images (680 patches corresponding to tree tops) all deep learning models were kept "frozen" during training. This stands for all the layers on the deep learning architectures except the final layers that output the classification category for each image remained unchanged during the whole training process. The idea behind this is that the pre-trained networks are already capable of adequately classifying our images and only a final layer that takes the output of the network and translates into the categories of our problem needs to be trained for each network. All networks were trained using different learning rates to give a broad view of their performance. Figure 8 contains Error Rate (ER) values for the validation set in each of the considered DL architectures over a list of learning rate values.

The figure shows how best results (0.096 ER) are obtained both by Resnet and Vgg. Densenet, Squeezenet and Squeezenet obtain slightly worse results with 0.11, 0.12 and 0.13 ER respectively. Resnet was consistently better than the other networks at this classification task. The values obtained show how these DL networks can adequately perform the classification task with a low rate of error. A more detailed look at the confusion matrix for LR 0.1 and the Resnet network (Table 4) shows how most classes are classified without error although some confusion can be observed for the Healthy Fir class. Specifically, it is confused in a few cases with the deciduous class (which does not represent a practical problem) and sometime healthy Fir trees are assigned the "sick Fir" category. This would be seen in a practical setting as a (small number of) false positive detection for an application aimed at detecting sick trees.

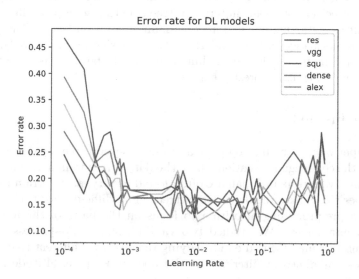

Fig. 8. Error Rate Results for tree classification for all learning rates and DL architectures.

Table 4. Confusion Matrix for the Tree health classification experiment.

Real Vs Predicted	Dead Fir	Deciduous	Healthy Fir	Sick Fir
Dead Fir	7	0	0	0
Deciduous	0	58	0	0
Healthy Fir	0	6	12	6
Sick Fir	0	1	0	45

While the current results show that deep learning is suitable for this type of classification task and represent a novel tool to aid the analysis of drone-acquired forest mosaics, improving the classification accuracy will be part of our future work. Specifically, larger networks will be considered along with larger datasets that can be used to train the full (unfrozen) networks.

4.4 Time Considerations

All experiments were run in a workstation using a Linux Ubuntu operating system with 10 dual-core 3 GHz processors and an NVIDIA GTX 1080 graphics card. With this setup, the average runtimes of the algorithms using their best combination of parameters for the eight DEM images show a high variability of performance. The fastest methods (considering the interest map pre-processing) are GMax (23 s), DBSCAN (62 s) and LMAX (102 s), while the slowest are KM (1537 s), GMM (1916 s) and FCM (5755 s). These results show how even the slower of them is faster than a human expert annotation. However, the algorithms have some precision problems in terms of tree counting so, a possibility is to use their result as a starting point to make human annotation faster. Consequently, both the performance metrics and these time considerations show how drone images and computer vision algorithms can already be used as a tool to save huge amounts of time by forestry experts.

5 Conclusions

In this paper we presented a complete analysis of several tree top detection algorithms in the challenging situation where the data comes from mixed forests that grow naturally. Forests in Japan are often found in very steep terrain presenting steep slopes this makes the detection of trees more difficult. For this reason, we designed a pre-processing algorithm to focus on the parts of the mosaic that actually contain trees. We studied two variants of this pre-process. The first built an interest map focused on identifying regions with different tree densities, the second was aimed at filtering out the floor using pixel altitude and color information.

On a subsequent step, six tree top detection algorithms were tested. These algorithms had their parameters adapted to the changing tree density conditions using the interest. Results showed how all algorithms were able to predict the tree top positions, (see Tables 2, 3). Gmax obtained best results with 90% of matching. FCM, GMM or DBSCAN reached accuracies over 80%. Regarding tree counting, Gmax obtained 8% in the tree counting criterion. Other methods obtained the following results: 11% (KM), 13–14% (FCM, GMM, DBSCAN). For completeness, we used the Hausdorff distance to measure the quality of the experiments (see Table 1). These results showed how the points predicted by GMax are not as close to the real tree tops as those predicted by GMM, KM or DBSCAN. These improved results that are also backed by qualitative observation. Taking into account all results shown, we conclude that the best algorithms for tree top detection, in terms of accuracy, are FCM, GM and DBSCAN. However, for a quick initial approach to the tree top positions, GMax showed the best performance (see Sect. 4.4).

In the final step of the presented pipeline, patches where extracted about tree tops and classified using five different deep learning architectures. Even though these networks where kept frozen due to the relatively low number (around 700) of tree tops considered and, thus, only the final layer of these networks was retrained, high classification accuracies were obtained (ER 0.096). The confusion matrix presented showed how clearly different classes were told apart without mistake and that mild confusion was observed for the "Sick Fir" class. In our future work we will improve classification accuracy by considering larger deep learning architectures trained unfrozen by using larger datasets. The use of data balancing and augmentation will also be explored.

Time consideration showed how the automatic algorithm studied provide forest scientists with new tools that can have an immediate impact in forest research. The algorithms presented make some of their tasks much faster than the existing alternative (fieldwork). Even if some error remains in the automatic approaches studied they can still be used as a good initial guess which can be corrected by the forest specialist in a matter of minutes for the applications where maximum precision is needed.

References

1. Agisoft: Agisoft metashape 1.5.5, professional edition. http://www.agisoft.com/downloads/installer/. Accessed 19 Aug 2019
2. Aliero, M., Bunza, M., Al-Doksi, J.: The usefulness of unmanned airborne vehicle (UAV) imagery for automated palm oil tree counting. J. For. **1** (2014)
3. Allen, C.D., Breshears, D.D.: Drought-induced shift of a forest–woodland ecotone: rapid landscape response to climate variation. Proc. Natl. Acad. Sci. **95**(25), 14839–14842 (1998)
4. Anderegg, W.R.L., Anderegg, L.D.L., Kerr, K.L., Trugman, A.T.: Widespread drought-induced tree mortality at dry range edges indicates that climate stress exceeds species' compensating mechanisms. Glob. Chang. Biol. **25**(11), 3793–3802 (2019)
5. Banu, T.P., Borlea, G.F., Banu, C.M.: The use of drones in forestry. J. Environ. Sci. Eng. **5** (2016)
6. Bezdek, J.C., Ehrlich, R., Full, W.: FCM: the fuzzy C-means clustering algorithm. Comput. Geosci. **10**(2), 191–203 (1984)
7. Bradski, G.: The OpenCV library. Dr. Dobb's J. Softw. Tools **25**, 120–125 (2000)
8. Chen, I.C., Hill, J.K., Ohlemüller, R., Roy, D.B., Thomas, C.D.: Rapid range shifts of species associated with high levels of climate warming. Science **333**(6045), 1024–1026 (2011)
9. Crimmins, S.M., Dobrowski, S.Z., Greenberg, J.A., Abatzoglou, J.T., Mynsberge, A.R.: Changes in climatic water balance drive downhill shifts in plant species' optimum elevations. Science **331**(6015), 324–327 (2011)
10. Csillik, O., Cherbini, J., Johnson, R., Lyons, A., Kelly, M.: Identification of citrus trees from unmanned aerial vehicle imagery using convolutional neural networks. Drones **2**(4), 39 (2018)

11. Danielsson, P.E., Seger, O.: Generalized and separable sobel operators. In: Machine Vision for Three-Dimensional Scenes, pp. 347–379. Elsevier (1990)

12. Díaz-Varela, R.A., De la Rosa, R., León, L., Zarco-Tejada, P.J.: High-resolution airborne UAV imagery to assess olive tree crown parameters using 3D photo reconstruction: application in breeding trials. Remote Sens. 7(4), 4213–4232 (2015)

13. Diez, Y., Kentsch, S., Lopez-Caceres, M.L., Nguyen, H.T., Serrano, D., Roure, F.: Comparison of algorithms for tree-top detection in drone image mosaics of Japanese mixed forests. In: Proceedings of the ICPRAM 2020. INSTICC, SciTePress (2020)

14. Diez, Y., Suzuki, T., Vila, M., Waki, K.: Computer vision and deep learning tools for the automatic processing of Wasan documents. In: Proceedings of the 8th International Conference on Pattern Recognition Applications and Methods - Volume 1: ICPRAM, pp. 757–765. INSTICC, SciTePress (2019)

15. Erikson, M., Olofsson, K.: Comparison of three individual tree crown detection methods. Mach. Vis. Appl. 16(4), 258–265 (2005)

16. Ester, M., Kriegel, H.P., Sander, J., Xu, X.: A density-based algorithm for discovering clusters in large spatial databases with noise. In: Proceedings of the KKD, vol. 96, pp. 226–231. AAAI Press (1996)

17. Falkowski, M.J., Smith, A.M., Gessler, P.E., Hudak, A.T., Vierling, L.A., Evans, J.S.: The influence of conifer forest canopy cover on the accuracy of two individual tree measurement algorithms using lidar data. Can. J. Remote. Sens. 34(sup2), S338–S350 (2008)

18. Frayer, W.E., Furnival, G.M.: Forest survey sampling designs: a history. J. For. 97(12), 4–10 (1999)

19. Gambella, F., et al.: Forest and UAV: a bibliometric review. Contemp. Eng. Sci. 9, 1359–1370 (2016)

20. García, E., et al.: Breast MRI and X-ray mammography registration using gradient values. Med. Image Anal. 54, 76–87 (2019)

21. Gougeon, F.A.: A crown-following approach to the automatic delineation of individual tree crowns in high spatial resolution aerial images. Can. J. Remote Sens. 21(3), 274–284 (1995)

22. Grotti, M., Chianucci, F., Puletti, N., Fardusi, M.J., Castaldi, C., Corona, P.: Spatio-temporal variability in structure and diversity in a semi-natural mixed oak-hornbeam floodplain forest. Ecol. Indic. 104, 576–587 (2019)

23. Guerra-Hernández, J., Cosenza, D.N., Rodriguez, L.C.E., Silva, M., Tomé, M., Díaz-Varela, R.A., Gonzáez-Ferreiro, E.: Comparison of ALS- and UAV(SfM)-derived high-density point clouds for individual tree detection in eucalyptus plantations. Int. J. Remote Sens. 39(15–16), 5211–5235 (2018)

24. Haralick, R.M., Shapiro, L.G.: Computer and Robot Vision, 1st edn. Addison-Wesley Longman Publishing Co., Inc., Boston (1992)

25. He, K., Zhang, X., Ren, S., Sun, J.: Deep residual learning for image recognition. CoRR abs/1512.03385 (2015)

26. Hirschmugl, M., Ofner, M., Raggam, J., Schardt, M.: Single tree detection in very high resolution remote sensing data. Remote Sens. Environ. 110(4), 533–544 (2007). ForestSAT Special Issue

27. Huang, G., Liu, Z., Weinberger, K.Q.: Densely connected convolutional networks. In: 2017 IEEE Conference on Computer Vision and Pattern Recognition (CVPR), pp. 2261–2269 (2016)

28. Iandola, F.N., Moskewicz, M.W., Ashraf, K., Han, S., Dally, W.J., Keutzer, K.: SqueezeNet: Alexnet-level accuracy with 50x fewer parameters and <1mb model size. CoRR abs/1602.07360 (2016)

29. Katoh, M., Gougeon, F.A.: Improving the precision of tree counting by combining tree detection with crown delineation and classification on homogeneity guided smoothed high resolution (50 cm) multispectral airborne digital data. Remote Sens. **4**(5), 1411–1424 (2012)
30. Ke, Y., Quackenbush, L.J.: A comparison of three methods for automatic tree crown detection and delineation from high spatial resolution imagery. Int. J. Remote Sens. **32**(13), 3625–3647 (2011)
31. Kelly, A.E., Goulden, M.L.: Rapid shifts in plant distribution with recent climate change. Proc. Natl. Acad. Sci. **105**(33), 11823–11826 (2008)
32. Kentsch, S., Lopez Caceres, M.L., Serrano, D., Roure, F., Diez, Y.: Computer vision and deep learning techniques for the analysis of drone-acquired forest images, a transfer learning study. Remote Sens. **12**(8), 1287 (2020)
33. Korpela, I., et al.: Single-tree forest inventory using lidar and aerial images for 3D treetop positioning, species recognition, height and crown width estimation. In: Proceedings of IAPRS, vol. 36 (2007)
34. Krizhevsky, A., Sutskever, I., Hinton, G.E.: ImageNet classification with deep convolutional neural networks. In: Proceedings of the 25th International Conference on Neural Information Processing Systems - Volume 1, NIPS 2012, pp. 1097–1105. Curran Associates Inc. (2012)
35. Larsen, M., Eriksson, M., Descombes, X., Perrin, G., Brandtberg, T., Gougeon, F.A.: Comparison of six individual tree crown detection algorithms evaluated under varying forest conditions. Int. J. Remote Sens. **32**(20), 5827–5852 (2011)
36. Lenoir, J., Gégout, J.C., Marquet, P.A., de Ruffray, P., Brisse, H.: A significant upward shift in plant species optimum elevation during the 20th century. Science **320**(5884), 1768–1771 (2008)
37. Li, W., Fu, H., Yu, L., Cracknell, A.: Deep learning based oil palm tree detection and counting for high-resolution remote sensing images. Remote Sens. **9**(1), 22 (2017)
38. Lloyd, S.: Least squares quantization in PCM. IEEE Trans. Inf. Theory **28**(2), 129–137 (1982)
39. Lopez, L., Hayashida, P., Mori, P., Koyama, P., Ashitani, P., Nobori, P.Y.: 8th forest plan. Internal Report (2014)
40. Mubin, N.A., Nadarajoo, E., Shafri, H.Z.M., Hamedianfar, A.: Young and mature oil palm tree detection and counting using convolutional neural network deep learning method. Int. J. Remote Sens. **40**(19), 7500–7515 (2019)
41. Natesan, S., Armenakis, C., Vepakomma, U.: ResNet-based tree species classification using UAV images. ISPRS Int. Arch. Photogramm. Remote. Sens. Spat. Inf. Sci. **XLII-2/W13**, 475–481 (2019)
42. Onishi, M., Ise, T.: Automatic classification of trees using a UAV onboard camera and deep learning. ArXiv abs/1804.10390 (2018)
43. Paneque-Gálvez, J., McCall, M.K., Napoletano, B.M., Wich, S.A., Koh, L.P.: Small drones for community-based forest monitoring: an assessment of their feasibility and potential in tropical areas. Forests **5**(6), 1481–1507 (2014)
44. Pedregosa, F., et al.: Scikit-learn: machine learning in Python. J. Mach. Learn. Res. **12**, 2825–2830 (2011)
45. Pinz, A.: Final results of the vision expert system VES: finding trees in aerial photographs. Wissensbasierte Mustererkennung. OCG-Schriftenreihe **49**, 90–111 (1989)
46. Pitkänen, J.: Individual tree detection in digital aerial images by combining locally adaptive binarization and local maxima methods. Can. J. For. Res. **31**(5), 832–844 (2001)

47. Pont, D., Kimberley, M.O., Brownlie, R.K., Sabatia, C.O., Watt, M.S.: Calibrated tree counting on remotely sensed images of planted forests. Int. J. Remote Sens. **36**(15), 3819–3836 (2015)

48. Pouliot, D., King, D., Bell, F., Pitt, D.: Automated tree crown detection and delineation in high-resolution digital camera imagery of coniferous forest regeneration. Remote Sens. Environ. **82**(2), 322–334 (2002)

49. Richardson, J.J., Moskal, L.M.: Strengths and limitations of assessing forest density and spatial configuration with aerial lidar. Remote Sens. Environ. **115**(10), 2640–2651 (2011)

50. Rizeei, H.M., Shafri, H.Z.M., Mohamoud, M., Pradhan, B., Kalantar, B.: Oil palm counting and age estimation from worldview-3 imagery and LiDAR data using an integrated OBIA height model and regression analysis. J. Sens. **2018**, 2536327:1–2536327:14 (2018)

51. Roure, F., Lladó, X., Salvi, J., Diez, Y.: GridDS: a hybrid data structure for residue computation in point set matching. Mach. Vis. Appl. **30**(2), 291–307 (2019)

52. Santoro, F., Tarantino, E., Figorito, B., Gualano, S., D'Onghia, A.M.: A tree counting algorithm for precision agriculture tasks. Int. J. Digit. Earth **6**(1), 94–102 (2013)

53. Shafri, H.Z.M., Hamdan, N., Saripan, M.I.: Semi-automatic detection and counting of oil palm trees from high spatial resolution airborne imagery. Int. J. Remote Sens. **32**(8), 2095–2115 (2011)

54. Shimada, T.: State of Japan's forests and forest management 2nd country report of Japan to the Montreal process. Forestry Agency, Japan, October 2009

55. Simonyan, K., Zisserman, A.: Very deep convolutional networks for large-scale image recognition. In: International Conference on Learning Representations (2015)

56. Srestasathiern, P., Rakwatin, P.: Oil palm tree detection with high resolution multispectral satellite imagery. Remote Sens. **6**(10), 9749–9774 (2014)

57. Torres-Sánchez, J., López-Granados, F., Serrano, N., Arquero, O., Peña, J.M.: High-throughput 3-D monitoring of agricultural-tree plantations with unmanned aerial vehicle (UAV) technology. PLoS ONE **10**, 1–20 (2015)

58. Torresan, C., et al.: Forestry applications of UAVs in Europe: a review. Int. J. Remote Sens. **38**(8–10), 2427–2447 (2017)

59. Van Rossum, G., Drake Jr., F.L.: Python tutorial. Centrum voor Wiskunde en Informatica Amsterdam, The Netherlands (1995)

60. Vauhkonen, J., et al.: Comparative testing of single-tree detection algorithms under different types of forest. For. Int. J. For. Res. **85**(1), 27–40 (10 2011)

61. Weinstein, B.G., Marconi, S., Bohlman, S., Zare, A., White, E.: Individual treecrown detection in RGB imagery using semi-supervised deep learning neural networks. Remote Sens. **11**(11) (2019)

Investigating Similarity Metrics
for Convolutional Neural Networks
in the Case of Unstructured Pruning

Alessio Ansuini$^{1(\boxtimes)}$ (iD), Eric Medvet$^{2(\boxtimes)}$ (iD), Felice Andrea Pellegrino$^{2(\boxtimes)}$ (iD),
and Marco Zullich$^{2(\boxtimes)}$ (iD)

^{1} Research and Technologies Institute, AREA Science Park, Trieste, Italy
`alessio.ansuini@areasciencepark.it`
^{2} Department of Engineering and Architecture, University of Trieste, Trieste, Italy
`{emedvet,fapellegrino}@units.it, marco.zullich@phd.units.it`

Abstract. Deep Neural Networks (DNNs) are essential tools of modern
science and technology. The current lack of explainability of their inner
workings and of principled ways to tame their architectural complexity
triggered a lot of research in recent years. There is hope that, by making
sense of representations in their hidden layers, we could collect insights on
how to reduce model complexity—without performance degradation—by
pruning useless connections. It is natural then to ask the following question: how similar are representations in pruned and unpruned models?
Even small insights could help in finding principled ways to design good
lightweight models, enabling significant savings of computation, memory, time and energy. In this work, we investigate empirically this problem on a wide spectrum of similarity measures, network architectures
and datasets. We find that the results depend critically on the similarity measure used and we discuss briefly the origin of these differences,
concluding that further investigations are required in order to make substantial advances.

Keywords: Machine learning · Pruning · Convolutional Neural
Networks · Lottery ticket hypothesis · Canonical correlation analysis ·
Centered kernel alignment · Network similarity · Explainable AI

1   Introduction

It is not fully understood why Deep Neural Networks (DNNs) generalize well to
new data also in conditions of severe overparametrization—in which the network
capacity would be enough to memorize large datasets—and what is the class of
functions that these networks are able to learn [1, 37]. In order to make sense of
inner workings of DNNs, in recent years many new methods have been introduced
with the purpose of comparing representations in trained networks and during
training [20, 28, 32]. On the other hand, recent pruning techniques proved very
effective in reducing big models to a tiny fraction of their original size, without

© Springer Nature Switzerland AG 2020
M. De Marsico et al. (Eds.): ICPRAM 2020, LNCS 12594, pp. 87–111, 2020.
https://doi.org/10.1007/978-3-030-66125-0_6

substantial degradation in performance [8,11,12,29]. These findings suggest that DNNs are able to represent data in effective ways also when they are forced to get rid of most of their parameters (up to more than 99%).

In the present exploratory work, we address, empirically, the following question: "How similar are representations in pruned and unpruned models?" We focus on Convolutional Neural Networks (CNNs) engaged in different Computer Vision tasks, training each model from scratch and pruning it with Iterative Magnitude Pruning (IMP) [16,29]. We then extract internal representations of the CNN layers and compare them by means of several recently introduced similarity measures.

The present work is an extension of [3], in which we trained multiple CNNs (from a single architectural family) on five subsets of increasing complexity of the dataset CIFAR-10 [21], pruning these networks using IMP. There, we observed a peculiar trend in the SVCCA similarity, particularly when we considered the complete dataset, from which we concluded that intermediate layers differ the most between pruned and unpruned networks; the following questions, however, remained unanswered:

- are these trends shared across datasets and architectures?
- how these trends depend on the particular notion of similarity used?

In the present work, we address these research questions by performing a more thorough experimental analysis w.r.t. [3] in terms of architectures, datasets, and similarity measures. We show that some of the most recently introduced similarity criteria, result in a remarkable stability of similarity across layers, thus suggesting that the action of IMP pruning (even when the resulting sub-network is much smaller than the original architecture) do not change substantially the representations. In order to make our findings reproducible and more accessible, we made the code publicly available at https://github.com/marcozullich/pruned_layer_similarity.

The remainder of the paper is organized as follows: in Sect. 2 we describe pruning techniques, stressing the innovations introduced in our investigation. In Sect. 3 we present in detail the employed techniques, namely, IMP and the similarity measures. In Sect. 4 we describe how these techniques are applied in this work, and provide a description of datasets, architectures, and hyperparameters. In Sect. 5 we describe our results on performance and layer-wise similarities between pruned and unpruned networks. Finally, in Sect. 6 we discuss critically our results, putting an accent on the difference of the results obtained with different similarity measures.

2 Related Work

2.1 Techniques for DNN Pruning

DNN pruning techniques may be split into two macro-categories [4]: unstructured and structured. Unstructured pruning acts without following "a specific geometry or constraint, [...] it leads to irregular sparsity". Structured pruning, on the contrary, acts on well-defined substructures of the DNN, such as a single neuron or a whole convolutional filter; IMP belongs to the first category [16]. In [29] various pruning techniques, both unstructured and structured, are compared on Computer Vision tasks; the authors show that unstructured pruning leads to the best outcomes, in particular IMP with *Learning Rate Rewind* (LRR), that we describe in Sect. 3.1 and use throughout the present work.

2.2   Comparisons Between Pruned and Unpruned DNNs

There exist several works analyzing analogies between pruned and unpruned DNNs. Apart from *performance* comparisons (test-set accuracy, time efficiency, energy consumption, *etc.*) which are the staple of the majority of such works, there is a minority of studies concentrating on other aspects.

Other types of comparison include, for instance, *calibration* [34] and *robustness* [35]; in [11] the *interpretability* of pruned CNNs w.r.t. their unpruned counterparts is considered.

Interpretability is related to the number of "convolutional units that recognize particular human-interpretable concepts", and it has been shown that pruning with IMP do not substantially alter interpretability. A more recent work compared *pruning masks* obtained from various pruning techniques, including IMP [26]. A pruning mask is a binary structure identifying with a 0 the parameters of the original DNN that have been pruned, and with a 1 the surviving ones. The authors compared masks using the Jaccard similarity (intersection-over-union). Although the relationship between representations and pruning masks is not immediate, the work provides interesting insights about the parallelisms between structured and unstructured pruning; moreover, the authors empirically show that, given an unpruned DNN, there exist multiple sub-networks that can match its test accuracy.

In our previous work [3], we addressed layer-wise similarities between pruned and unpruned DNNs using a similarity metric specifically designed for neural networks, Mean CCA Similarity [28] (see also Sect. 3.2). We are not aware of other works dedicated to layer-by-layer comparisons of pruned and unpruned DNNs.

3   Tools

In this section we present the tools we used to perform our experiments: IMP—together with the main strategies for its application—and the similarity metrics used to compare representations.

3.1   IMP

IMP, first proposed in [16], is a pruning technique that iteratively performs the following three steps: (1) start from a fully trained neural network (*complete* or *unpruned network*), (2) prune parameters with magnitude falling below a given quantile, (3) re-train the network with the remaining parameters for a given number of epochs.

At each iteration, IMP produces a network with increased sparsity, i.e., with a larger portion of weights set to 0.

Several variants on this theme are possible, based on how to choose the parameters to be removed:

- *Global Pruning* [12]: all the parameters are pooled together and a given proportion of them is pruned, regardless of the layer they belong to.
- *Local Pruning* [12]: a fixed proportion of low-magnitude parameters is pruned from each layer; the threshold is determined layer-by-layer.
- *Mixed Pruning* [38]: a hybrid between global and local pruning—parameters may be pooled in separate structures depending on the layer they belong to, and pruning may be applied separately for each pool. For instance, in [38] the authors experiment with pooling separately parameters from convolutional layers and fully-connected layers.

In [24] it was shown that global pruning outperforms, in terms of test-set accuracy, the other two strategies; hence, in this work, we will use the former.

When IMP was introduced, it was customary to re-train the pruned neural network for a small number of iterations (*fine-tuning*, FT) while keeping the Learning Rate (LR) fixed at the same value as the last epoch of training of the complete network. Since then, this procedure has been shown [29] to produce subpar results as far as accuracy is concerned. Additional heuristics for re-training were introduced in subsequent works:

- *Weight Rewind* (WR) [12]: before re-training, *rewind* the surviving parameters to their configuration at initialization. This strategy showed promising results, albeit only on relatively small architectures; it was later found in [13] that rewinding at a configuration of a training iteration *close* to the initial one (*late resetting* strategy) allowed for the successful application of WR also on larger networks, such as VGG19 [30].
- *Learning Rate Rewind* (LRR) [29]: before re-training, do not modify the value of the surviving parameters, but re-use the same LR schedule that was used in the complete network. The authors also brought empirical evidence that LRR produces networks having better accuracy than WR and FT, especially at higher pruning rates.

In [3], we employed IMP with WR and late resetting. In the present work, we decided to switch to IMP with LRR, due to its better empirical results. As we will later note in Sect. 5, if we restrict our considerations on SVCCA, the results we get are comparable to the ones obtained in [3], suggesting that, as far as the representations of the layers of the neural networks are concerned, there is not much difference between IMP with WR and IMP with LRR.

3.2 Similarity Metrics for Neural Networks Data Representations

In this section, we present the various metrics to compare representations in the (hidden) layers of neural networks which we employed in this work.

These metrics allow 'for the comparison between generic layers of neural networks (possibly belonging to different architectures) through the *representations*, i.e., the *activation matrices* obtained as output of such layers in response to a fixed dataset [28]. For a dataset composed by n data points, a generic fully-connected layer of p neurons is hence represented by an $n \times p$ matrix.

Comparing Layers with *Convolutional Structure*. We say that a layer has a convolutional structure when its representation is not two-dimensional, as is the case of fully-connected layers, but four-dimensional. For instance, convolutional layers and two-dimensional max-pooling layers fall under this category.

Generally, we can represent such layers with four-dimensional tensors having shape $n \times c \times h \times w$, where n is the number of data points through which we obtain the representation, c is the number of channels in the layer, and h and w are the *spatial dimensions* of the data point at the layer[1].

Since the metrics that we are going to present work with matrices, additional strategies for treating these tensors are needed in order to produce a two-dimensional matrix out of the original four-dimensional tensor. These strategies might differ from metric to metric.

The present work is focused on CNNs operating on two-dimensional images, thus we will not consider strategies to compare layers whose representations have larger dimensions (e.g., three-dimensional convolutions).

Metrics Based on Canonical Correlation Analysis (CCA). CCA [18] is a multivariate statistical technique to compare two representations of phenomena described starting from the same dataset of n units. CCA finds two linear transforms such that, when applied to the two representations, produce a set of orthonormal vectors in a common space, and these vectors have maximum pair-wise Pearson correlation. In our case, the phenomena are the two layers we wish to compare.

Formally, given two matrices L_1, L_2 such that $L_1 \in \mathbb{R}^{n \times p_1}$ and $L_2 \in \mathbb{R}^{n \times p_2}$, let $\tilde{p}$ be the minimum between p_1 and p_2. The two sought transforms are called $W_1 \in \mathbb{R}^{p_1 \times \tilde{p}}$ and $W_2 \in \mathbb{R}^{p_2 \times \tilde{p}}$.

By applying them to $L1$ and $L2$, we get

$$Z_1 = L_1 W_1 \tag{1}$$
$$Z_2 = L_2 W_2, \tag{2}$$

with $Z_1, Z_2 \in \mathbb{R}^{n \times \tilde{p}}$. Denoting by $z_i^{(1)}$ the i-th column of Z_1 (also called the i-th *canonical vector*), we wish that:

---

[1] For *spatial dimension* we mean the size of each single channel of the image (or analogous two-dimensional structure) after the application of the convolutions operated by the given layer.

(a) $z_i^{(k)} \perp z_j^{(k)}$, with $k \in \{1,2\}, i,j \in \{1,\ldots,\tilde{p}\}, i \neq j$, and

(b) the pair $z_i^{(1)}, z_i^{(2)}$, with $i \in \{1,\ldots,\tilde{p}\}$ maximizes the residual Pearson correlation, called *canonical correlation* (CC), identified by ρ_i.

Hence, we obtain a sequence of column vectors pairs $(z_i^{(1)}, z_i^{(2)})_{i \in \{1,\ldots,\tilde{p}\}}$ exhibiting decreasing CCs.

Mean CCA Similarity. These values of CC may be averaged [28] to obtain a similarity metric called **Mean CCA Similarity**:

$$\text{Mean CCA Similarity}(L_1, L_2) \doteq \frac{\sum_{i=1}^{\tilde{p}} \rho_i}{\tilde{p}} \tag{3}$$

The CCs may actually be obtained [33] in a one-shot fashion from the Singular Value Decomposition (SVD), applied to a matrix derived from the variance-covariance matrices of the two layers L_1, L_2.

SVCCA. The Singular Vector Canonical Correlation Analysis (SVCCA), was proposed in [28]. The idea behind this technique is to perform a SVD for dimensionality reduction of the representation of the layers, then operate the CCA as explained in the previous section. The authors of [28] recommend to apply SVD such that only the singular values accounting for the 99% of variance are retained.

Such a dimensionality reduction is motivated by the observation that, in layers representations, "many low variance directions (neurons) are primarily noise". Moreover, the SVD is expected to reduce overestimation of the similarity on some degenerate configurations for the layers.

The Mean CCA Similarity calculated when using SVCCA will be referred to as **Mean SVCCA Similarity**.

PWCCA. In [23], it was argued that the Mean CCA Similarity may misrepresent the similarity between two layers, given the fact that all the correlation coefficients in Eq. (3) are weighted equally. It was then proposed to weigh the CCs according to the contribution of the corresponding canonical vectors in determining the representation of the original layer.

We recall that $L_1 \in \mathbb{R}^{n \times p_1}$ and $L_2 \in \mathbb{R}^{n \times p_2}$ are the layers representation. We call $l_m^{(1)} \in \mathbb{R}^n$ the m-th column vector of L_1. It contains the activations of the m-th neuron to all the n data points. We suppose, without loss of generality, that $p_1 \leq p_2$, so that $\tilde{p} = \min(p_1, p_2) = p_1$. The canonical vectors of L_1, $z_i^{(1)} \in \mathbb{R}^n$, are the column vectors of $Z_1 = L_1 W_1$. Then, the contribution α_i of $z_i^{(1)}$ in determining L_1 is:

$$\alpha_i \doteq \sum_{j=1}^{p_1} |l_j^T z_i^{(1)}| \tag{4}$$

where ^{T} denotes transposition. In case $p_2 < p_1$, Eq. (4) must be formulated using the corresponding indices and vectors from L_2 instead of L_1.

Plugging the contributions as weights of the mean in Eq. (3), we get the target similarity metric, called PWCCA (Projection Weighted Canonical Correlation Analysis):

$$\text{PWCCA}(L_1, L_2) \doteq \frac{\sum_{i=1}^{\tilde{p}} \alpha_i \rho_i}{\sum_{i=1}^{\tilde{p}} \alpha_i} \tag{5}$$

Handling of Layers with Convolutional Structure. When comparing layers with convolutional structure, whose representation is a 4D tensor, the tensors are reshaped as in [28]. Precisely, given $L_1 \in \mathbb{R}^{n \times c \times h \times w}$, the spatial dimensions h and w are *merged* into the first dimension (the one concerning the data points), thus yielding a matrix $\tilde{L}_1 \in \mathbb{R}^{nhw \times c}$. The reason for this reshaping is that, as noted in [28], the *degrees of freedom* of neurons in layers with convolutional structures are limited, due to the spatial structure of the filters, to the channel only. Incidentally, the reshaping tackles the issue raised in [20] that, when the number of data points is smaller than the number of neurons, CCA-based similarity metrics produce inappropriate results. Indeed, usually, despite $n < chw$, it also happens that $nhw > c$: thus, in such case, the reshaping produces representations where the number of data points is larger than the number of neurons.

This procedure has a major limitation concerning the comparison between layers having different spatial dimensions. Let's suppose that the two layers have spatial dimensions $h \times w$ and $h' \times w'$ respectively (with c and c' channels respectively), the corresponding representations, reshaped as above, have size $nhw \times c$ and $nh'w' \times c'$. Since a requirement for CCA is that the number of rows must be the same between the two representations (i.e., the number of data points in the representations of the two layer must be the same), it follows that the metrics based on CCA cannot be obtained in this case. Similarly, it is also impossible to compare, e.g., a convolutional layer with a fully-connected layer.

Though, to our knowledge, the existing literature has not proposed solutions to this problem, the authors of [28] and [23] have rendered their code and consequent considerations public in [14], while proposing two techniques to enable the comparison: (a) interpolation, to upsample the smaller image such that it matches the larger image spatial dimensions, and (b) average pooling along the spatial dimensions, to *average out* the two spatial dimensions and obtain a matrix of shape $n \times c$. We remark that we will not be needing these metrics, since we will always be comparing convolutional and max-pooling layers having the same number of data points and the same spatial dimensions.

3.3 Kernel-Based Metrics

Metrics based on kernels are computed from the Gram matrices obtained from the representations of the layers. In a sense, these techniques consider an additional step from those based on CCA, viewing the representation of the layer not as the activation matrix L, but as the Gram matrix obtained from applying a kernel function κ to the rows of L itself.

Centered Kernel Alignment (CKA). CKA [6,7] is a similarity metric for kernels computed from representations obtained from the same number of data points n. [20] makes the case for CKA as a similarity index particularly suitable for comparing DNNs layers representations. The authors cite the invariance to orthogonal transformations and isotropic scalings of the space as desirable properties enjoyed by CKA.

We consider once again our two layers representations $L_1 \in \mathbb{R}^{n \times p_1}$ and $L_2 \in \mathbb{R}^{n \times p_2}$, with corresponding Gram matrices $K_1 \in \mathbb{R}^{n \times n}$ and $K_2 \in \mathbb{R}^{n \times n}$, both positive semi-definite and obtained out of universal kernel functions κ_1 and κ_2. We constrain L_1, L_2 to be centered w.r.t. their column means[2] or, alternatively, their Gram matrices K_1, K_2 must be centered by subtracting both the column and row means[3].

CKA is calculated as:

$$\mathrm{CKA}(K_1, K_2) \doteq \frac{\langle K_1, K_2 \rangle_F}{\|K_1\|_F \|K_2\|_F} \tag{6}$$

where $\|K\|_F = \sqrt{\mathrm{tr}(KK^T)}$ is the Frobenius norm, and $\langle K_1, K_2 \rangle_F = \mathrm{tr}(K_1 K_2^T)$ is the Frobenius inner product.

CKA itself is a normalization[4] of the Hilbert-Schmidt Independence Criterion [15] to test the independence between sets of random variables.

In [20], it is argued that CKA is a metric which is fitter than CCA-based similarities to compare DNN representations. Besides the aforementioned invariances, the authors base this claim upon two experiments in which they record much greater success by CKA in recognizing similarity patterns in architecturally equivalent DNNs trained from different random initializations.

Normalized Bures Similarity (NBS). A more recent work [32], proposes, in addition to CKA, the use of another metric based on Gram matrices, NBS [5]. Still, the requirement is that L_1, L_2, or K_1, K_2, must be centered as explained for CKA.

It is calculated as:

$$\mathrm{NBS}(K_1, K_2) = \frac{\sqrt{\mathrm{tr}(K_1^{1/2} K_2 K_1^{1/2})}}{\sqrt{\mathrm{tr}\, K_1 \, \mathrm{tr}\, K_2}} \tag{7}$$

Also this quantity is comprised between 0 and 1. [32] refers to it as an alternative to CKA, sharing all of its invariances. It is to be noted, though, that the authors argue, on limited settings, that this metric may be inferior w.r.t. CKA.

Considerations on Kernels. Both CKA and NBS are, in their respective works, calculated on Gram matrices obtained with linear kernels or variations of them.

---

[2] I.e., for each column, its mean across the instances must be 0.
[3] I.e., for each row/column, its mean across the columns/rows must be 0.
[4] Such that its value lies between 0 and 1.

In [20], some experiments are conducted with Radial Basis Function kernels, finding that results obtained with these kernels are similar with respect to linear kernels, preferring the latter due to their simplicity and absence of tunable parameters. Taking this into account, we will also calculate CKA and NBS using linear kernels only.

In [32], only a variation of a linear kernel is used. This kernel is modified in order to incorporate the gradient of the DNN. They do so by calculating Gram matrices on (a) the values of the parameters of the layer, (b) the values of the gradient of the loss function w.r.t. the parameters of the layer, and combining the two via the Hadamard product (matrix element-by-element product) obtaining a new positive semidefinite Gram matrix. While we believe that this technique may be well suited to compute similarities of DNNs in their training steps, we think that gradients are not needed in order to compare feature maps of fully-trained networks, although it may be interesting to incorporate this metric in future analyses. We will hence conform to work with Gram matrices obtained strictly on the parameter space.

4   Methods

In order to carry out our exploration, we operated following this scheme:

1. We trained a *complete* (unpruned) CNN on a given dataset and a given optimizer until convergence.
2. We pruned it using IMP with LRR for 20 iterations with a pruning rate of 20%. This value is suggested as a default in [29]. The pruning was operated for P runs, each time re-starting from the same complete CNN. We averaged the similarities over these runs in order to get more robust results. After the execution of IMP for 20 iterations, the pruned CNNs have a sparsity level of around 98.5%[5] (or, alternatively, around 1.5% of the parameters survive the pruning operation).
3. We obtained the representations for the hidden layers of all the CNNs, both unpruned and pruned.
4. We compared, using multiple similarity metrics, each layer of the pruned CNNs with the corresponding layer of the complete CNN.

We repeated this process over different datasets and CNN architectures:

- CNN on the dataset CIFAR-10 [21]; architecture based on VGG16 [30].
- CNN on the dataset CIFAR-10; architecture based on ResNet [17].
- CNN on the dataset SVHN [25]; architecture based on VGG [30].

The details about the datasets, the CNN architectures, and the optimizers used are presented in Sects. 4.1 and 4.2. The metrics employed in the comparison are Mean SVCCA Similarity, PWCCA, CKA, and NBS.

---

[5] The exact value depends on the presence of layers or parameters not affected by pruning, such as batch normalization.

4.1 Datasets

CIFAR-10. CIFAR-10 [21] is a dataset for image classification composed of 60000 color images having size 32×32 pixels. The images belong to 10 classes, of which 6 are animals and the other 4 are means of transportation. The dataset, which is available on https://www.cs.toronto.edu/~kriz/cifar.html, is already split into a training set composed of 50000 images and a test-set of 10000 images.

In our experiments, the dataset was augmented by applying random data augmentation schemes (cropping, horizontal flipping, affine transformation, cutout).

SVHN. SVHN [25] is a dataset composed of 99289 color images of size 32×32 pixels, each exhibiting a caption of a house number extracted from the online service Google Street View of Google Maps[6]. Each image is centered into a single digit, which is the target of the classification. Hence, there are 10 classes (digits from 0 to 9). Some images may exhibit more than one digit: in this case, only the central digit must be considered and the other digits act as distractors. The dataset, which is available on http://ufldl.stanford.edu/housenumbers/, is already split into a training set of 73257 images and a test-set of 26032 images. Moreover, an additional dataset of 531131 images may be used for training purposes (e.g., as a validation dataset) although it is specified in the hosting site that these examples are "somewhat less difficult".

SVHN is currently available both as an image classification dataset and as an object recognition dataset. In this second case, the images are larger than 32×32 and the target is to recognize all of the digits present inside the images. In this work, we refer to SVHN solely as an image classification dataset.

4.2 CNN Architectures and Optimizers Used

VGG. [30] is a relatively simple family of CNN architectures characterized by a cascade of *convolutional blocks* followed by fully-connected layers and the output layer, having as many neurons as the number of classes. Each convolutional block is composed of 2, 3, or 4 convolutional layers having the same number of filters (usually doubling the number of filters of the convolutional layers of the previous block), followed by a final max-pooling layer.

VGG16 for CIFAR-10. VGG16 is a specification of VGG with 5 convolutional blocks.

The original implementation uses the ReLU activation function for all the hidden layers and has 2 fully-connected hidden layers at the end; moreover, no dropout [31] or batch normalization (BN) [19] are employed. Our implementation differs from the original one, tracing the recent work on IMP (see [29]):

---

[6] https://maps.google.com.

- we employ BN before the activation function in each convolutional layer;
- we drop the two fully-connected layers, thus rendering the CNN fully convolutional [22]. After the last max-pooling layer, Global Average Pooling (GAP) is applied to flatten the output of said layer and feed it to the output layer.

We will refer to this network architecture as *VGG16_BN* throughout this work: a schematic representation of VGG16_BN is present in Fig. 1.

VGG16_BN was trained for 160 epochs on CIFAR-10 using the optimizer Stochastic Gradient Descent with Momentum [27] (SGDM) and employing a step decay LR annealing schedule. The hyperparameters are as of [29], with a batch size of 128 since we trained the models on a single GPU.

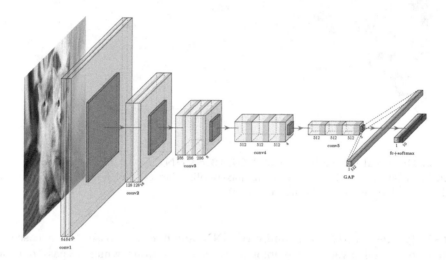

Fig. 1. Graphical schematization of **VGG16_BN**. Yellow blocks represent convolutional layers, red blocks represent max-pooling layers, and teal blocks represent fully-connected layers. (Color figure online)

VGG for SVHN. In order to train a CNN on SVHN, we employed a custom VGG composed of 4 blocks, each one having two convolutional layers, except for the last one. In the first block each convolutional layer has 32 filters. The number of filters double in each convolutional block, so that the convolutional layer in the fourth block has 256 filters. After the last block, the output is pooled with GAP and fed to the output layer, thus rendering also this CNN fully-convolutional. In this work, we will refer to this architecture as *VGG_SVHN*: a schematic representation of VGG_SVHN is shown in Fig. 2.

We trained the network for 15 epochs with a batch size of 50, we used the optimizer SGDM with hyperparameters as for VGG16_BN, and a step decay LR schedule, annealing by a factor of 10 at epochs 7 and 12.

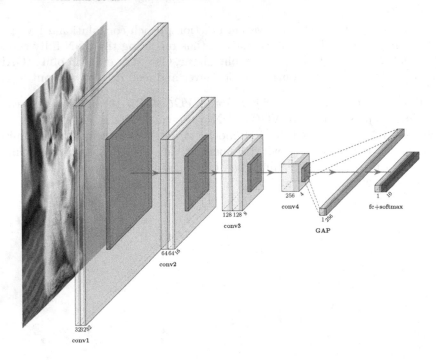

Fig. 2. Graphical schematization of **VGG16_SVHN**. Yellow blocks represent convolutional layers, red blocks represent max-pooling layers, and teal blocks represent fully-connected layers. (Color figure online)

ResNet. ResNet [17] is a family of CNN architectures based on a cascade of convolutional layers and employing *skip connections* which bypass one or more convolutional layers. Skip connections propagate the received information content directly to the end of the skipped layers. The output of the skipped layers is then summed to the content propagated by the skip connections: for this reason, the skipped layers can be also considered as belonging to a *residual block*, while the corresponding skip connection may also be called *identity shortcut*. The skipped connections allow for the construction of very deep DNNs, tackling the vanishing gradient problem.

We trained a variation of a ResNet on CIFAR-10. The architecture is inspired by a publicly available GitHub implementation (https://github.com/davidcpage/CIFAR-10-fast); a scheme is reported in Fig. 3.

The main difference between this architecture and the classic ResNet is that the second convolutional block (conv2 in Fig. 3) has no subsequent residual block. According to the author of this architecture, this allows for a better optimization on CIFAR-10; generally, the convergence of this CNN is very fast and it allows for a full training in less than 10 minutes on a single GPU. Due to this reason, we will refer to this architecture as *ResNet_fast*.

We trained this CNN for 24 epochs and batch size of 512 using SGDM with LARS updates [36], as in the original implementation of this network.

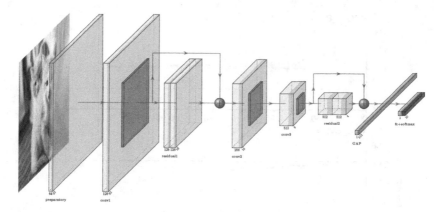

Fig. 3. Graphical schematization of **ResNet_fast**. Yellow blocks represent convolutional layers, red blocks represent max-pooling layers, and teal blocks represent fully-connected layers. (Color figure online)

5 Results

5.1 Test-Set Accuracy

The performances in terms of test-set accuracy are shown in Fig. 4.

We can note how the two models based upon CIFAR-10 (VGG16_BN and ResNet_fast) behave similarly: the first iterations of IMP produce CNNs which outperform the complete model; at around 10% of parameters remaining, the accuracy spikes, then it slowly decreases, while remaining comparable w.r.t. the unpruned counterpart. This behaviour is expected from a DNN pruned with IMP, and has been known since [12].

Focusing instead on the CNN trained on SVHN (VGG_SVHN), we note a different behaviour: somewhat unexpectedly, the test-set accuracy of all the pruned networks tends to decrease as IMP is performed. This may be an indication that the unpruned structure of the network (VGG_SVHN) is adequate w.r.t. the difficulty of the problem (SVHN) and pruning even a small percentage of the connections is detrimental to its generalization capability. It may also be that the hyperparameters of the optimizer are adequate to train the complete network only, and may be hence tuned during the following IMP iterations to improve accuracy. We are not going to delve into this analysis as we believe it is not relevant to the foundations of this work. Anyway, this trend in test-set accuracy on SVHN was noticed also in other works, such as [34], albeit on different CNN architecture.

5.2 Layer-Wise Pruned vs. Unpruned Similarity

As stated in Sect. 4, we compared the layers of the pruned CNNs with their unpruned counterparts. Specifically, the comparison was operated on representations of:

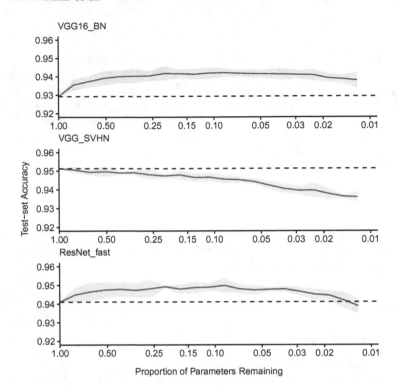

Fig. 4. Test-set accuracy averaged over multiple runs for our three models. Error bands correspond to 2 standard deviations. The dotted lines represent the reference accuracy of the complete model (corresponding to proportion of parameters equals to 1.00). The x-axis is in logarithmic scale.

- convolutional layers (in short, *conv*; *conv_res* if the layer is part of a residual block of a ResNet), *after* the application of BN and activation function (ReLU);
- max-pooling layers (in short, *pool*);
- for ResNet only, addition nodes (in short, *add*), i.e., the nodes where the residuals are summed to the output of the skipped connections;
- output layers (in short, *out*), *before* the application of the activation function (softmax).

VGG16_BN. The values of the metrics for VGG16_BN are shown in Fig. 5. We can make the following observations.

Mean SVCCA Similarity and PWCCA show a very specific "U" shape which we also noted in [3][7] with simpler CNN architectures, while the problem was still CIFAR-10. The curves still bottom out around the third convolutional block,

---

[7] In that work, we employed Mean SVCCA Similarity only, but the shape produced by PWCCA is very similar.

with a minimum slightly greater than 0.3. In addition to that, we can tell that the similarities decrease as the IMP iteration is increased, a phenomenon which become slightly less obvious as we near the output layer. Finally, in all iterations, the representations of the output layer have a similarity larger than 0.9.

CKA tells a different story: overall, the similarity is still high for all layers; while in SVCCA and PWCCA we had a similarity index ranging from 0.3 to around 0.95, in CKA we never record a value lower than 0.75. Moreover, the general trend we can observe is that the similarity seems to decrease as we progress from the first layers toward the output layer. Within the first two convolutional blocks, the similarity is rather packed between different iterations, with slightly smaller values as the IMP iteration is increased; after that, the values fan out, and the CNNs with higher sparsity exhibit a smaller similarity w.r.t. the unpruned counterparts. It is also of interest to note that the output layers seem to be not as similar as indicated in SVCCA/PWCCA; moreover, the values seem to be largely more scattered, ranging from around 0.77 to 0.95. Furthermore, starting with the 8-th IMP iteration (around 16% of parameters remaining in the model), they stack together CKA-wise, exhibiting a similarity of around 79%.

The values produced by NBS seem to blend characteristics of both CKA and SVCCA/PWCCA: the values range from 0.7 to 1.0, similarly to what we observed in CKA, and there is a "fan-out" effect at the third convolutional block, akin to CKA. On the other hand, we may notice that there does not seem to be the overall decreasing trend produced by CKA; instead, there is a clear bottom, identifiable between the 3-rd pooling layer and the subsequent convolutional layers, after which the similarities increase once again. This parallels what happens with SVCCA and PWCCA, although, in that case, the similarities were much lower, closer to 0.35, while with NBS they rest between 0.7 and 0.85. Finally the output layers exhibit a higher NBS than they do with CKA; on the other hand, there still seems to be a convergence at around 0.9 for the sparser CNNs.

VGG_SVHN. Figure 6 shows the results for VGG_SVHN. W.r.t. VGG16_BN, we see more consistency between the four metrics.

Mean SVCCA Similarity and PWCCA do not exhibit a minimum with a clear subsequent recovery; instead, in both cases there seems to be two bottoms in the 3-rd and the 4-th convolutional blocks, after which the similarity spikes at the output; despite this spike, there seems not to be a recovery in the similarity corresponding to subsequent hidden layers, as instead we noticed with VGG16_BN.

CKA shows a similar landscape w.r.t. VGG16_BN, with an overall decreasing trend leading to the output layer; moreover, there is a noticeable bowl for the last 3 or 4 iterations of IMP in correspondence with the 3-rd pooling layer. Again, we can note somewhat of a large range of values at the output layer, with CKA values ranging from 0.78 to 0.95.

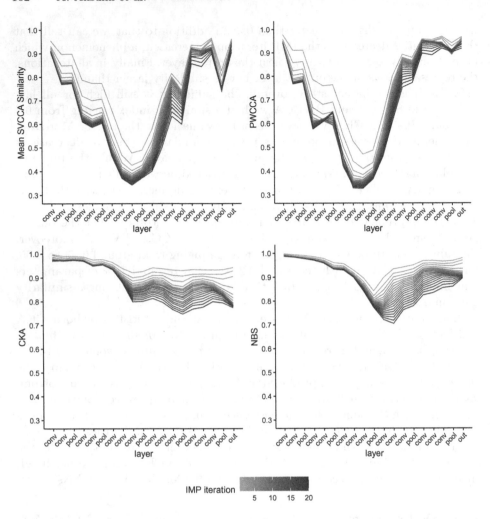

Fig. 5. Average layer-wise similarity between layers of pruned **VGG16_BN** vs. unpruned counterpart for various metrics (indicated on the y-axis). The values are averages over 20 runs of IMP. Error bands omitted for chart readability. Line color (light to dark) identifies the iteration of IMP.

Finally, the figure traced by NBS is very similar to CKA, barring the "bowl" at the 3-rd convolutional block we saw in CKA: hence we might say that NBS seems a more regular CKA counterpart.

5.3   ResNet_fast

The similarity values for ResNet_fast are shown in n Fig. 7.

CKA and PWCCA show a trend which, at first sight, may recall the one saw in VGG16_BN. It must be noted, though, that, excluding the output layer,

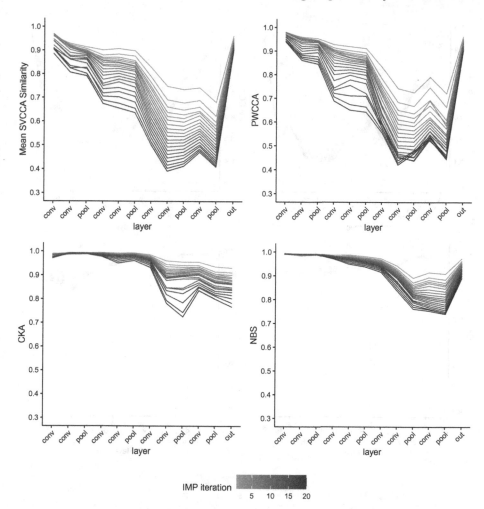

Fig. 6. Average layer-wise similarity between layers of pruned **VGG_SVHN** vs. unpruned counterpart for various metrics (indicated on the y-axis). The values are averages over 5 runs of IMP. Error bands omitted for chart readability. Line color (light to dark) identifies the iteration of IMP.

the recovery in similarity is very weak after the minimum found at the third convolutional layer. Moreover, the similarity is slightly higher w.r.t. VGG16_BN: for VGG16_BN, the bottom reached as low as 0.35 for SVCCA and 0.32 for PWCCA, while for ResNet_fast the values are always above 0.40, and even above 0.45 for PWCCA. In addition to this, there seems to be a clear convergence of the similarity values as the IMP iteration (and, hence, the sparsity of the CNN) increases, a phenomenon that did not seem as evident in the other two networks.

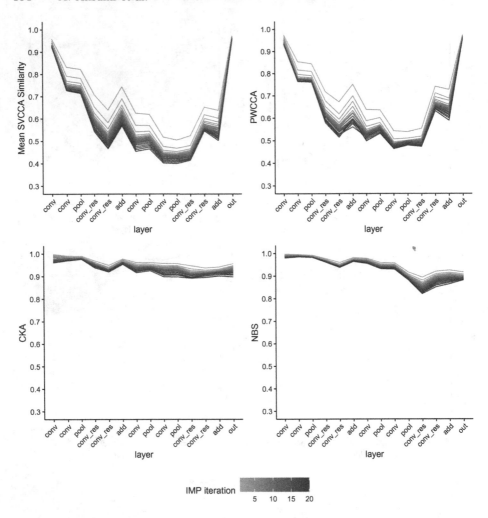

Fig. 7. Average layer-wise similarity between layers of pruned **ResNet_fast** vs. unpruned counterpart for various metrics (indicated on the y-axis). The values are averages over 5 runs of IMP. Error bands omitted for chart readability. Line color (light to dark) identifies the iteration of IMP.

For CKA and NBS, again the similarity values are all very high, with CKA hardly touching the 0.90 mark, while NBS reaches as low as 0.82. Generally, CKA seems to exhibit no trend at all, with values remaining about constant. NBS, on the other hand, shows a more distinct trend, with a minimum located at the second residual block, with a slight recovery as we head toward the output layer.

6   Discussion

6.1   Takeaways from Results

The results presented in Sect. 5.2 show that the four similarity metrics we used to compare representations in CNNs lead to different outcomes. While CCA-based metrics reveal a "U"-shaped trend, CKA gives constant or slightly decreasing similarities; finally, NBS outputs a "U"-shaped similarity profile with some peculiar traits: (a) the minimum is reached 2–3 layers "later" w.r.t CCA-based metrics and (b) the similarity is much higher w.r.t. SVCCA or PWCCA.

In [3] we conjectured that the trend observed with Mean SVCCA Similarity could be a consequence of the Intrinsic Dimensionality (ID) of representations [2]: since in intermediate layers the ID is typically at its highest (often much higher than the ID of the input), there might be the possibility that in intermediate layers there is more variability and therefore more opportunities for dissimilarities that could be captured by such measures.

In the light of these new results, however, this conjecture seems problematic since (a) CKA suggests a very different picture than SVCCA or PWCCA, and (b) NBS, despite in qualitative agreement with SVCCA and PWCCA, places the minimum further in the progression of the layers, where the ID is typically far from its maximum [2].

In [20, 32] it is argued that CKA is to be preferred to other CCA-based measures, since the latter pose too stringent requirements (invariance to invertible linear transformations) that can lead to paradoxical results.

The similarity results obtained with CKA seem to suggest the following:

a) representations in pruned and unpruned networks are remarkably similar;
b) there is a weak but progressive decrease of similarity (i) as we increase the sparsity in the CNN, and (ii) as we transverse the network in the forward direction; however, this trend seems not to be very pronounced, and there are typically plateaus in the CKA similarity.

We did not compare explicitly the features learnt by the CNNs, although an analysis may be possible considering, for instance (i) parameters-based similarity measures instead of representation-based, or (ii) quantitative metrics comparing features learnt by the DNNs, like Net2Vec [10].

6.2   Comparing Output Layers

Conversely to hidden layers, it could be argued that a similarity metric to compare output layers does not need invariances to orthogonal transformation, since the role of the neurons within the output layers are fixed: in a DNN for classification, neuron i of the output layer is proportional to the probability of assignment of a given data point to the i-th class.

The four metrics we used up to now have all been indicated as fit to compare DNNs for a given amount of reasons: invariances to specified transformations, measuring statistical correlations between random variables in different dimensions, *etc.* As an addition to our analysis, we experiment with comparing the output layers with a slight variation of a classical similarity metric for vectors: the cosine similarity. Given vectors $a, b \in \mathbb{R}^p$, the cosine similarity is defined as

$$\text{csim}(a, b) = \frac{a^T b}{\|a\|_2 \|b\|_2} \tag{8}$$

This similarity metric is used to compare generic vectors belonging to the same space. An output layer of c neurons, though, is represented a generic matrix $A \in \mathbb{R}^{n \times c}$ where n is the number of data points employed to obtain the representation. In order to enable the comparison between two output layers A, B via cosine similarity, we simply consider the vectorized representations $\text{vec}(A) = [A_{11}, \dots, A_{1c}, \dots, A_{n1}, \dots, A_{nc}]$ and feed it into Eq. 8. Finally, since $\text{csim}(\cdot, \cdot) \in [-1, 1]$, in order to normalize its support w.r.t. the other four metrics used, we consider its magnitude:

$$|\text{csim}(\text{vec}(A), \text{vec}(B))| \in [0, 1]$$

This adjustment reflects already what happens, for instance, in CKA, which, to put it simply, measures the (in)dependence between two sets of variables [20], but does not distinguish whether the possible dependence is positive or negative, being comprised between 0 and 1.

Settings and Results. We evaluated the network VGG16_BN with the same subset of CIFAR-10 of 5000 data points (see Sect. 4), keeping only the representations of the output layer. The evaluation was repeated for the complete network and all of the pruned networks (20 runs × 20 IMP iterations).

The results of this similarity compared with the previous four are shown in Fig. 8. We note that:

a) the vectorized cosine similarity does not exhibit the "stacking" effect we note on the last iterations of IMP; conversely, the values seem rather well distributed along the range $[0.80, 0.97]$;
b) unlike SVCCA, PWCCA, and NBS, which all record similarities above 0.9, the cosine similarity starts high at the first iterations, before sinking to around 0.8. Under this facet, it seems more akin to CKA, even if the distribution w.r.t. the iteration of IMP is different. Note also that the cosine similarity and CKA are somewhat related as CKA is based upon the Hilbert-Schmidt Independence Criterion, which is itself based upon the cosine similarity between features of a representation [20].

The fact that we notice some differences between output layers may indicate how, despite producing DNNs with comparable test-set accuracy, the probabilities of assignment of the 5000 data points to the various classes in the pruned models may disagree w.r.t. the unpruned model. This may be attributable, for example, to a difference in calibrations, as noted in [34].

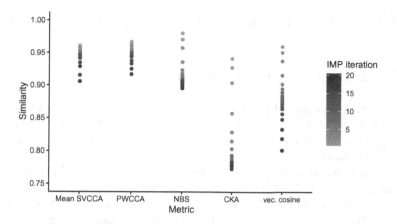

Fig. 8. Average similarity of pruned output layers w.r.t. the unpruned counterparts for the network **VGG16_BN**, for various iterations of IMP and different similarity metrics. Values are averaged over 20 different runs of IMP starting from the same complete network.

6.3   Considerations on the Rotational Invariance of Similarity Metrics for Convolutional Layers

To wrap up the discussions, we believe it is of interest to make a brief digression whether the rotational invariance is really a desirable property that a generic similarity metric must possess. It is undeniable that this property be enjoyed for comparing, for instance, fully-connected layers: if a network is composed only of such layers, it may be possible to carefully permute all of the neurons in its hidden layers to obtain a new DNN producing the exact same output; in this case, we wish that a similarity metric indicates that the layers of the old and the new network are pairwise identical.

This, instead, is not the case for CNNs, because the parameters of convolutional layers possess a spatial constraint w.r.t. the image they see: neurons inside a channel of a convolutional layer recognize specific features that they would not be able to distinguish as accurately if "moved around" in other positions within the same channel. The same does not hold, instead, when we consider full channels: a careful permutation of the channels in a CNN, along with the neurons in the possible fully-connected layers, can result in a CNN producing the same output.

Hence, we argue that, for the case of convolutional layers (and pooling layers as well, as they share the same spatial structure), a similarity metric should enjoy a rotational invariance only at the level of channels of convolutional layers. In Sect. 3.2, when talking about the handling of convolutional layers by SVCCA and PWCCA, we reported that, to compute similarities for convolutional layers, these two metrics require a preprocessing step for the layers such that the spatial dimensions are *merged* into the data points dimension, leaving as *proper neurons* in the representation the sole dimension regarding channels. This strategy may also be, in principle, applicable to CKA and NBS and may be analyzed in a future work.

7   Conclusions and Future Work

In this work, we compared representations in pruned and unpruned networks, trained for Computer Vision task, extending in several directions the range of our earlier work [3], by considering a wider spectrum of similarity measures, new models and datasets.

Specifically, we analyzed layer-wise representation similarities across several CNN architectures trained on CIFAR-10 and SVHN. We considered a representative set of available similarity measures, namely: Mean SVCCA Similarity, PWCCA, CKA, and NBS. These metrics produce, in our settings, contrasting results which do not allow to draw univocal conclusions on the impact of pruning on representations.

While SVCCA and PWCCA yield similar results, suggesting that in pruned network intermediate layers create very dissimilar representations with respect to the complete network (see Figs. 5 to 7, panels on the first row), CKA shows a weak, almost monotonic decrease across the network (see Figs. 5 to 7, left panel on the second row). NBS, which in principle is similar to CKA, and shares its desirable invariances, is in qualitative agreement with the trends exhibited by SVCCA and PWCCA, on a much smaller scale. All the similarity measures we investigated are in agreement in indicating a progressive departure—as more and more connections are removed during the iterations of IMP—from the original representations. In the case of CKA anyway, this departure is contained (similarity never falling below 0.75 in all our experiments).

We proposed two observations on the rotational-invariance of metrics for comparing output layers and convolutional layers, respectively, hinting at directions for future works (see Sect. 6.3). Very recently, a modification of existing similarity measures was proposed, integrating the information coming from the gradient [32].

We identified several directions for further research on comparing representations in pruned and unpruned networks:

- exploration of new similarity measures that integrate CKA with the information coming from gradients [32];
- modifications of existing metrics, e.g., enforcing channels-only rotational-invariance in convolutional layers;
- extensions to large-scale datasets, like ImageNet [9];
- exploration of other pruning strategies, like structured pruning or Accelerated IMP [39], to examine how representations obtained in this way differ w.r.t. IMP with WR.

A detailed understanding of representations in pruned networks is of primary importance for theoretical and practical reasons. We hope that this exploratory, empirical work will inspire new theoretical investigations on the nature of these representations, enabling a deeper understanding of the inner workings of deep neural networks, and enhancing the security of their applications.

References

1. Allen-Zhu, Z., Li, Y., Liang, Y.: Learning and generalization in overparameterized neural networks, going beyond two layers. In: Advances in Neural Information Processing Systems, pp. 6155–6166 (2019)
2. Ansuini, A., Laio, A., Macke, J.H., Zoccolan, D.: Intrinsic dimension of data representations in deep neural networks. In: NIPS 2019 (2019)
3. Ansuini, A., Medvet, E., Pellegrino, F.A., Zullich, M.: On the similarity between hidden layers of pruned and unpruned convolutional neural networks. In: De Marsico, M., Sanniti di Baja, G., Fred, A. (eds.) Proceedings of the 9th International Conference on Pattern Recognition Applications and Methods (ICPRAM 2020), pp. 52–59. Scitepress, La Valletta, February 2020
4. Anwar, S., Hwang, K., Sung, W.: Structured pruning of deep convolutional neural networks. ACM J. Emerg. Technol. Comput. Syst. (JETC) **13**(3), 1–18 (2017)
5. Bures, D.: An extension of Kakutani's theorem on infinite product measures to the tensor product of semifinite w*-algebras. Trans. Am. Math. Soc. **135**, 199–212 (1969)
6. Cortes, C., Mohri, M., Rostamizadeh, A.: Algorithms for learning kernels based on centered alignment. J. Mach. Learn. Res. **13**, 795–828 (2012)
7. Cristianini, N., Shawe-Taylor, J., Elisseeff, A., Kandola, J.S.: On kernel-target alignment. In: Advances in Neural Information Processing Systems, pp. 367–373 (2002)
8. Crowley, E.J., Turner, J., Storkey, A., O'Boyle, M.: Pruning neural networks: is it time to nip it in the bud? arXiv preprint arXiv:1810.04622 (2018)
9. Deng, J., Dong, W., Socher, R., Li, L.J., Li, K., Fei-Fei, L.: ImageNet: a large-scale hierarchical image database. In: CVPR 2009 (2009)
10. Fong, R., Vedaldi, A.: Net2vec: quantifying and explaining how concepts are encoded by filters in deep neural networks. In: Proceedings of the IEEE Conference on Computer Vision and Pattern Recognition, pp. 8730–8738 (2018)
11. Frankle, J., Bau, D.: Dissecting pruned neural networks. arXiv preprint arXiv:1907.00262 (2019)
12. Frankle, J., Carbin, M.: The lottery ticket hypothesis: Finding sparse, trainable neural networks. In: International Conference on Learning Representations (2019). https://openreview.net/forum?id=rJl-b3RcF7
13. Frankle, J., Dziugaite, G.K., Roy, D.M., Carbin, M.: Stabilizing the lottery ticket hypothesis. arXiv preprint arXiv:1903.01611 (2019)
14. Google: (sv)cca for representational insights in deep neural networks (2019). https://github.com/google/svcca
15. Gretton, A., Bousquet, O., Smola, A., Schölkopf, B.: Measuring statistical dependence with Hilbert-Schmidt norms. In: Jain, S., Simon, H.U., Tomita, E. (eds.) ALT 2005. LNCS (LNAI), vol. 3734, pp. 63–77. Springer, Heidelberg (2005). https://doi.org/10.1007/11564089_7
16. Han, S., Pool, J., Tran, J., Dally, W.: Learning both weights and connections for efficient neural network. In: Cortes, C., Lawrence, N.D., Lee, D.D., Sugiyama, M., Garnett, R. (eds.) Advances in Neural Information Processing Systems, vol. 28, pp. 1135–1143. Curran Associates, Inc. (2015)

17. He, K., Zhang, X., Ren, S., Sun, J.: Deep residual learning for image recognition. In: Proceedings of the IEEE Conference on Computer Vision and Pattern Recognition, pp. 770–778 (2016)
18. Hotelling, H.: Relations between two sets of variates. Biometrika **28**(3–4), 321–377 (1936). https://doi.org/10.1093/biomet/28.3-4.321
19. Ioffe, S., Szegedy, C.: Batch normalization: accelerating deep network training by reducing internal covariate shift. In: ICML, pp. 448–456 (2015). http://proceedings.mlr.press/v37/ioffe15.html
20. Kornblith, S., Norouzi, M., Lee, H., Hinton, G.: Similarity of neural network representations revisited. In: Chaudhuri, K., Salakhutdinov, R. (eds.) Proceedings of the 36th International Conference on Machine Learning. Proceedings of Machine Learning Research, vol. 97, pp. 3519–3529. PMLR, Long Beach, California, USA, 09–15 June 2019. http://proceedings.mlr.press/v97/kornblith19a.html
21. Krizhevsky, A., Hinton, G., et al.: Learning multiple layers of features from tiny images (2009)
22. Long, J., Shelhamer, E., Darrell, T.: Fully convolutional networks for semantic segmentation. In: Proceedings of the IEEE Conference on Computer Vision and Pattern Recognition, pp. 3431–3440 (2015)
23. Morcos, A., Raghu, M., Bengio, S.: Insights on representational similarity in neural networks with canonical correlation. In: Bengio, S., Wallach, H., Larochelle, H., Grauman, K., Cesa-Bianchi, N., Garnett, R. (eds.) Advances in Neural Information Processing Systems, vol. 31, pp. 5732–5741. Curran Associates, Inc. (2018)
24. Morcos, A., Yu, H., Paganini, M., Tian, Y.: One ticket to win them all: generalizing lottery ticket initializations across datasets and optimizers. In: Wallach, H., Larochelle, H., Beygelzimer, A., d'Alché Buc, F., Fox, E., Garnett, R. (eds.) Advances in Neural Information Processing Systems, vol. 32, pp. 4932–4942. Curran Associates, Inc. (2019)
25. Netzer, Y., Wang, T., Coates, A., Bissacco, A., Wu, B., Ng, A.Y.: Reading digits in natural images with unsupervised feature learning (2011)
26. Paganini, M., Forde, J.: On iterative neural network pruning, reinitialization, and the similarity of masks. arXiv preprint arXiv:2001.05050 (2020)
27. Qian, N.: On the momentum term in gradient descent learning algorithms. Neural Netw. **12**(1), 145–151 (1999)
28. Raghu, M., Gilmer, J., Yosinski, J., Sohl-Dickstein, J.: SVCCA: singular vector canonical correlation analysis for deep learning dynamics and interpretability. In: Guyon, I., et al. (eds.) Advances in Neural Information Processing Systems, vol. 30, pp. 6076–6085. Curran Associates, Inc. (2017)
29. Renda, A., Frankle, J., Carbin, M.: Comparing fine-tuning and rewinding in neural network pruning. In: International Conference on Learning Representations (2020)
30. Simonyan, K., Zisserman, A.: Very deep convolutional networks for large-scale image recognition. arXiv preprint arXiv:1409.1556, September 2014
31. Srivastava, N., Hinton, G., Krizhevsky, A., Sutskever, I., Salakhutdinov, R.: Dropout: a simple way to prevent neural networks from overfitting. J. Mach. Learn. Res. **15**(1), 1929–1958 (2014)
32. Tang, S., Maddox, W.J., Dickens, C., Diethe, T., Damianou, A.: Similarity of neural networks with gradients. arXiv preprint arXiv:2003.11498 (2020)
33. Uurtio, V., Monteiro, J.M., Kandola, J., Shawe-Taylor, J., Fernandez-Reyes, D., Rousu, J.: A tutorial on canonical correlation methods. ACM Comput. Surv. **50**(6) (2017). DOIurl10.1145/3136624

34. Venkatesh, B., Thiagarajan, J.J., Thopalli, K., Sattigeri, P.: Calibrate and prune: improving reliability of lottery tickets through prediction calibration. arXiv preprint arXiv:2002.03875 (2020)
35. Ye, S., et al.: Adversarial robustness vs. model compression, or both. In: The IEEE International Conference on Computer Vision (ICCV), vol. 2 (2019)
36. You, Y., Gitman, I., Ginsburg, B.: Large batch training of convolutional networks. arXiv preprint arXiv:1708.03888 (2017)
37. Zhang, C., Bengio, S., Hardt, M., Recht, B., Vinyals, O.: Understanding deep learning requires rethinking generalization. arXiv preprint arXiv:1611.03530 (2016)
38. Zhou, H., Lan, J., Liu, R., Yosinski, J.: Deconstructing lottery tickets: zeros, signs, and the supermask. In: Advances in Neural Information Processing Systems, pp. 3597–3607 (2019)
39. Zullich, M., Medvet, E., Pellegrino, F.A., Ansuini, A.: Speeding-up pruning for artificial neural networks: introducing accelerated iterative magnitude pruning. In: Proceedings of the 25th International Conference on Pattern Recognition (2021)

Encoding of Indefinite Proximity Data: A Structure Preserving Perspective

Maximilian Münch[1,2(✉)], Christoph Raab[1,3], and Frank-Michael Schleif[1]

[1] Department of Computer Science, University of Applied Sciences Würzburg-Schweinfurt,
97074 Würzburg, Germany
{maximilian.muench,christoph.raab,frank-michael.schleif}@fhws.de
[2] Bernoulli Institute for Mathematics, C. & S. and AI, University of Groningen, P.O. Box 407,
9700 AK Groningen, The Netherlands
[3] Bielefeld University, CITEC, 33619 Bielefeld, Germany

Abstract. Over the last two decades, kernel learning attracted enormous interest and led to the development of a variety of successful machine learning models. The selection of an efficient data representation is one of the critical aspects to get high-quality results. In a variety of domains, this is achieved by incorporating expert knowledge in the used domain-specific similarity measure. The majority of machine learning models require the similarity measure to obey some mathematical constraints. In particular to be a valid Mercer kernel, the similarity function that is used as a kernel function, has to be symmetric and positive semi-definite. Domain-specific similarity functions can be made available to kernel machines by additional operations from the field of indefinite learning. Approaches used today are often inefficient and harmful to the domain encoded knowledge. In this paper, we analyze multiple approaches in indefinite learning and suggest a novel, efficient preprocessing operation which widely preserves the domain-specific information, while still providing a Mercer kernel function. In particular, we address practical aspects like out of sample extension and an effective implementation of the approach. This is accompanied by extensive experimental results on various typical data sets with superior results in the field.

Keywords: Non-metric · Proximity learning · Similarity · Indefinite · von Mises iteration · Eigenvalue correction · Shifting · Flipping · Clipping

1 Introduction

In various natural and social sciences, large data sets have an intrinsic complex structure. Examples are sequential data like protein- or genome-sequences, graph structures, time series or text corpora. These so-called structured data are compositional and it is very challenging to represent the respective samples by a fixed-length vector encoding [42].

Therefore, another representation by means of domain-specific pairwise proximities is frequently employed. The proximities can either be measured by similarities, most related to kernel functions, or by dissimilarities, related to distance functions. In this context, *similarities* describe how close or similar two data points and *dissimilarity*

© Springer Nature Switzerland AG 2020
M. De Marsico et al. (Eds.): ICPRAM 2020, LNCS 12594, pp. 112–137, 2020.
https://doi.org/10.1007/978-3-030-66125-0_7

measures indicate how different two elements are to each other. Note that an associated similarity measure can always be derived for a given symmetric dissimilarity, as shown later on. Depending on the type and the mathematical properties of the proximity function, either distance-based models like the classic k-nearest neighbor algorithm or similarity-based models like kernel machines are used. The most popular model using similarities by means of metric inner products is the support vector machine [53].

Due to the compositional nature of the data, classical similarity measures like the Euclidean inner product or dissimilarity measures like the Euclidean distance, are not applicable, in general. The more generic proximity measures are effective from the domain perspective but violate mathematical requirements given classical machine learning algorithms [41]. Also an embedding into a vector space is challenging and often suboptimal [41]. The field of indefinite learning provides concepts to enable the use of classical learning machines for these more generic types of proximities [51].

Today, such similarity or distance measures are quite common in various disciplines: for example in bioinformatics, various alignment functions such as the Smith-Waterman algorithm [20] or Dynamic Time Warping [47] are used for sequential data.

Also in the area of object computer vision, various proximity measures, such as the tangent distance [48], shape matching distance or pyramid match kernel are used. Furthermore, such measures find application in medicine, economics, psychology, and many other disciplines. A list of measures and domains is given in Table 1. One of the main reasons for the creation of such a variety of new proximity measures is their degree of accuracy: domain-specific measures or functions allow a more accurate representation of the relationships among data points than standard measures such as Euclidean distance [13,42]. In the creation of the data representation, substantial domain expertise has often been incorporated directly, such that the expected discriminating properties of the objects are directly considered and are already essential part of the proximity relationship.

Table 1. List of commonly used non-metric proximity measures in various domains.

Measure	Application field
Dynamic time warping (DTW) [47]	Time series or spectral alignment
Inner distance [31]	Shape retrieval e.g. in robotics
Compression distance [10]	Generic used also for text analysis
Smith Waterman alignment [20]	Bioinformatics
Divergence measures [9]	Spectroscopy and audio processing
Generalized Lp norm [30]	Time series analysis
Non-metric modified Hausdorff [11]	Template matching
(Domain-specific) alignment score [35]	Mass spectrometry

However, domain-specific proximity measures do not fulfill desirable mathematical properties. In particular, the (associated) similarity measure is often not positive (semi-) definite (*non-psd*), implying that the measure cannot be directly used in classical kernel approaches. For dissimilarity based approaches, metric properties are also often required [41]. These so-called *indefinite* matrices pose a severe problem for many machine learning algorithms since they violate common mathematical assumptions of the optimization procedures used to fit the model or in the structure of the algorithm itself. For example, the very effective support vector machine can only be used to a limited extent, since the convexity of the optimization can no longer be guaranteed [33]. In case of a psd input matrix, the underlying convex optimization can be solved by standard numerical solvers, approaching the global optimum [44]. However, if the input matrix is indefinite, there might be no global minimum or either only a local optimum is found or the solver does not converge at all [33]. Employing a non-psd measure in SVM is, therefore, a heuristic approach without any guarantees, which becomes prohibitive in practical applications.

Consequently, strategies and techniques that can handle non-metric proximity measures are desirable. For this purpose, a considerable variety of approaches that can process indefinite data has been published - see [33,51] for an extended discussion. However, some of these approaches modify the structure of the data significantly, resulting in the partial destruction of the data's natural properties.

In this contribution, we discuss and detail a recently published approach by [37], referred to as *advanced shift*, that transforms indefinite data into psd while preserving large parts of the data's topology. In Sect. 2, we provide relevant notation, review the most prominent indefinite learning strategies and discuss their advantages and disadvantages. Subsequently, we provide an in-depth analysis of the novel advanced shift approach for non-metric proximity data and show further practical findings and additional in-depth experiments. We conclude by a detailed discussion and provide an outlook to further research in this area.

2   Non-metric Proximity-Based Learning

In this section, we provide a brief overview of the concepts of learning with non-metric proximity data and potential ways to deal with indefinite data. Additionally, we also point out considerable limitations of the previously proposed methods.

2.1   Notation and Basic Concepts

Kernels and Kernel Functions. Let X be a collection of N objects x_i, $i = 1, 2, ..., N$, in some input space. Further, let $\phi : X \mapsto \mathcal{H}$ be a mapping of patterns from X to a high-dimensional or infinite-dimensional Hilbert space $\mathcal{H}$ equipped with the inner product $\langle \cdot, \cdot \rangle_{\mathcal{H}}$. The transformation ϕ is, in general, a non-linear mapping to a high-dimensional space $\mathcal{H}$ and may commonly not be given in an explicit form. Instead of this a kernel function $k : X \times X \mapsto \mathbb{R}$ is given which encodes the inner product in $\mathcal{H}$. The kernel k is a positive (semi) definite function such that $k(x,x') = \langle \phi(x)^\top, \phi(x') \rangle$ for any $x, x' \in X$. The matrix $K := \Phi^\top \Phi$ is an $N \times N$ kernel matrix derived from the training data, where $\Phi : [\phi(x_1), \ldots, \phi(x_N)]$ is a matrix of images (column vectors) of the training data in $\mathcal{H}$.

The motivation for such an embedding comes with the hope that the non-linear transformation of input data into higher dimensional $\mathcal{H}$ allows for using linear techniques in $\mathcal{H}$. Kernelized methods process the embedded data points in a feature space utilizing only the inner products $\langle \cdot, \cdot \rangle_{\mathcal{H}}$ (kernel trick) [53], without the need to calculate ϕ explicitly. The specific kernel function can be very generic, but in general, it is expected that the kernel is a Mercer kernel [53]. Most prominent are the linear kernel with $k(x, x') = x^\top x'$ as the Euclidean inner product or the RBF kernel $k(x, x') = \exp\left(-\frac{\|x-x'\|^2}{2\sigma^2}\right)$, with σ as a free parameter. Although the kernel function can be very generic, nearly all common kernel methods assume the kernel to satisfy Mercer's conditions [53] and thus be positive semi-definite (psd). However, as already mentioned, these conditions are not always fulfilled, particularly with the use of domain-specific similarity measures. Their pairwise proximity (similarity or dissimilarity) measures can be conveniently summarized in an $N \times N$ (symmetric) proximity matrix with no restriction if the given proximities are exclusively determined by measures for similarity or dissimilarity.

If a generic similarity measure is used (or a non-metric dissimilarity), negative eigenvalues occur and the data are represented in a so-called Krein space, consisting of two Hilbert spaces. A Krein space can be interpreted as an *indefinite* inner product space endowed with a Hilbertian topology [2]. An inner product space $(\mathcal{K}, \langle \cdot, \cdot \rangle_{\mathcal{K}})$ is a Krein space if we have two Hilbert spaces $\mathcal{H}_+$ and $\mathcal{H}_-$ spanning $\mathcal{K}$ such that $\forall f \in \mathcal{K}$ we have $f = f_+ + f_-$ with $f_+ \in \mathcal{H}_+$ and $f_- \in \mathcal{H}_-$ and $\forall f, g \in \mathcal{K}$, $\langle f, g \rangle_{\mathcal{K}} = \langle f_+, g_+ \rangle_{\mathcal{H}_+} - \langle f_-, g_- \rangle_{\mathcal{H}_-}$. When working in the Krein space, the need is no longer to minimize the loss of standard kernel algorithms but rather stabilize the loss in average [33].

We refer to proximity matrices created on a similarity measure as S and proximity matrices based on a measure of dissimilarity as D, respectively. A conversion from D to a corresponding S can be realized by a process referred to as double centering [41]. Models which do not employ an explicit vector space but similarities only are also referred to as similarity based learning [13]. In [17] and [40], the authors outlined this to be also applicable to indefinite proximities with low computational costs. Subsequently, we focus exclusively on kernel-based *supervised* learning (in particular classification) and will consider only similarities.

2.2 Indefinite Proximities

Learning a classifier needs not to be done using vectorial data but can solely based on a proximity representation, as mentioned before. If the underlying measure is a generic similarity function (in contrast to a Mercer kernel), we work with non-psd or indefinite kernels [51] and dedicated algorithms. Otherwise, additional preprocessing operations are required to train an accurate model with this data.

Employing a data representation in form of proximities is particularly helpful in the following scenarios: (a) the original data is not available in vectorial form, e.g. protein sequences, graph data, text data or (b) the primal focus is on the relationship between the data points [13]. As outlined in [41], the majority of analysis algorithms are applicable only in a tight mathematical setting, in particular the metric properties are often required. Although this may sound like a promising strategy at first, the restriction to metrics imposes major disadvanatages. While the scientific world is widely metric, in reality, many problems are better addressed by proximity measures that neglect these metric restrictions for a better information representation [49]. In [11], a modified non-metric version of the Hausdorff distance was performed that outperformed the original metric Hausdorff distance in the context of object matching in images.

Also, it is evident that some data are inherently compositional and cannot be represented by a metric without loss of information. This is the case for graphs, text documents, spectral data, or biological data [8,28,39]. Modern embedding techniques based on autoencoder methods still try to approximate reliable embeddings into a vectorial space, are hard to fit and require enormous amounts of resources, which is not always available and these techniques have shown high performance only for narrow domains, like text processing in a particular language [18,56,57]. Alternatives are often restricted to metric spaces [54], which requires correction techniques for non-metric data as detailed later on. The application of domain-specific measures, already effective over many decades, does not require such efforts and has shown superior performance in many cases [13]. For this reason, multiple authors criticized these limitations and clearly pointed out that these non-metric parts of the data contain valuable information and should be preserved [41,49]. For this purpose, several approaches have been proposed to address the problem of indefinite proximity learning as schematically shown in Fig. 1. There are two main directions that allow to work with non-metric proximity data despite the problems of indefiniteness. The two main lines for working with non-metric data are completely opposite:

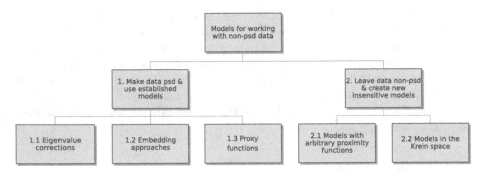

Fig. 1. Overview on various approaches to address the problem of non-psd proximity data based on [51].

1) Make Data psd and Use Established Models: The data is modified to become psd. Afterwards, models can be used which have a solid theoretical basis and which have been used successfully for years. The structure of the data should be preserved, otherwise there is a risk of information loss. Basically, there are three considerable subcategories in which the psd-transformation approaches can be divided:

Eigenvalue Corrections: As metric violations lead to negative eigenvalues in the data's eigenspectrum, some approaches simply tried to modify the data's eigenspectrum.

The intention is to modify the negative eigenvalues in such a way that no negative eigenvalues remain after the correction. These correction procedures will be discussed in more detail later on.

Embedding Approaches: Embeddings are another way to transform non-metric or non-psd input data to an equivalent metric representation. Here, the main purpose is to find a description of the data in another (but metric) vector space that preserves the proximities of the data as well as possible. In general, the data are embedded in a Euclidean space since many classifiers assume the Euclidean metric anyway, either implicitly or explicitly. However, especially with non-metric input data, exact embeddings are rarely feasible, as already outlined before. For this reason, it is common to embed the data in a Pseudo-Euclidean space. See [22,41] for an extended discussion.

Learning a Proxy Function: Learning a proxy function over the input proximity data was one of the first approaches to transform non-metric to metric data. Over the years, several ways were suggested to obtain an alternate psd-matrix that is maximally aligned to the non-psd input data (see [51] for an overview).

2) Leave Data Non-psd and Create New Insensitive Models: An alternative way is to keep the data non-psd and to create models that are insensitive to indefiniteness. Thus, the original structure of the data and also the information in the negative parts of the eigenspectrum remain exactly the same. However, the negative eigenspectrum has to be considered in the optimization processing leading to computational complex and rarely sparse solutions.

Learning of Indefinite Decision Functions: Here, the model definition is based directly on the nonmetric proximity function. In [3], properties of similarity functions are discussed that have to be satisfied to ensure good capabilities for a learning task. There it is assumed that the similarity matrix is reinterpreted as an empirical feature space. Recent algorithms with a decision function based on nonmetric proximities are given in [1,7,27].

Learning Models in the Krein Space: The last group of approaches in this list keeps the data unchanged and makes use of a reformulation from an optimization into a stabilization problem by means of an extension of the common inner product in the Reproducing Kernel Hilbert Space (RKHS) into a Reproducing Kernel Krein space (RKKS) [33]. In [33], this is used to establish a valid SVM model, named KSVM, in the RKKS. This KSVM approach is able to work directly on the indefinite kernel matrices and outperformed all other methods available at that time. Recent extensions of this idea have been proposed in [50,52].

The aim of this subsection was to give an overview of some possibilities of how to handle non-psd data in general. Although there are several methods that directly work with indefinite data, these models are not frequently used. This is mainly due to their quadratic to cubic complexity and the obtained complex, non-sparse models. Also the stability, induced by the eigendecomposition in Krein spaces, sometimes results in some difficulties [32,33]. Therefore, we focus in the following on eigenspectrum corrections that can be done without reformulating the entire optimization framework.

2.3 Eigenspectrum Corrections

As discussed in the previous section, a natural way to address the indefiniteness problem is to correct the eigenspectrum of S, to obtain a positive semi-definite matrix S^*.
Since metric violations cause negative eigenvalues in the eigenspectrum of the matrix
S, the matrix becomes non-metric. To correct S, a generic approach is to use an eigendecomposition: $S = U \Lambda U^\top$, where Λ contains the eigenvalues λ_i corresponding to the
eigenvectors u_i in U.

Now, the eigenvalues in Λ can be modified in order to remove all negative parts
in the eigenspectrum by different strategies, leading to Λ^*. After the application of an
appropriate correction procedure on the eigenvalues, an approximated (but now psd)
matrix can be reconstructed, referred to as $S^* = U \Lambda^* U^\top$. Common strategies for modifying the negative eigenvalues include *flipping, clipping, squaring*, and *shifting*, which
are illustrated in Fig. 2. Here, x-axis represents the index of the eigenvalue while the
y-axis illustrates the value of the eigenvalue (referred to as impact or strength). The
red line shows the original magnitude of the eigenvalue, the blue-dashed line shows the
impact after the correction method.

The data in Fig. 2(a) illustrates the eigenvalues of an artificial sample data set. The
data set consists of negative and positive eigenvalues, with an equal contribution on
the eigenspectrum. On the left side of Fig. 2(a), the eigenvalues $\lambda < 0$ are shown in
orange. On the right side, the positive eigenvalues $\lambda > 0$ are highlighted in green. In the
following, various correction methods and their impact on the eigenvalues' contribution
on the whole eigenspectrum are considered.

Flip Eigenvalue Correction: The flip operation was one of the earliest correction techniques used to achieve positive semi-definiteness. For this purpose, all negative eigen-
values in Λ are set to $\lambda_i := |\lambda_i| \ \forall i$. The motivation behind this approach is to retain
some of the information coded in the negative eigenvalues [19,43]. Figure 2(b) displays
the preservation of potentially relevant information lying in the negative eigenvalues
of the original data. Consequently, the impact of the originally negative eigenvalues
remains intact [41]. This operation can be calculated with $O(N^3)$ or $O(N^2)$ if low-rank
approaches are used.

Square Eigenvalue Correction: All negative eigenvalues in Λ are set to $\lambda_i := \lambda_i^2 \ \forall i$
which amplifies large and shrink very small eigenvalues. The square eigenvalue correc-
tion can be achieved by matrix multiplication [55] with $\approx O(N^{2.8})$. A major drawback
of this method, however, is that large eigenvalues increase even further, whereas small
eigenvalues may vanish completely. The small eigenvalues in Fig. 2(c) seem almost
negligible compared to the impact of the other eigenvalues.

Clip Eigenvalue Correction: This approach comes with the hope that all negative eigenvalues are caused by noise and hence can be eliminated without loss of information. All
negative eigenvalues in Λ are set to 0 (see Fig. 2(d)). Following [23], this clipping
operation leads to the nearest psd matrix S in terms of the Frobenius norm. Such a correction can be achieved by an eigendecomposition of the matrix S, a clipping operator

on the eigenvalues, and the subsequent reconstruction. This operation has a complexity of $O(N^3)$. The complexity might be reduced by either a low-rank approximation or the approach shown by [34] with roughly quadratic complexity.

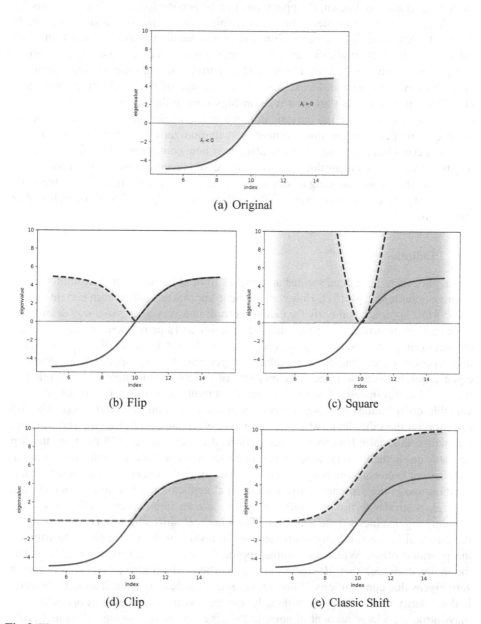

(a) Original

(b) Flip

(c) Square

(d) Clip

(e) Classic Shift

Fig. 2. Eigenspectrum plots of a generated example. Plot 2(a) shows the original spectrum of the eigenvalues of this exemplary dataset. Plots 2(d)–2(e) show the impact of the respective correction method on the eigenvalues.

Classical Shift Eigenvalue Correction: The shift operation was already discussed earlier by different researchers [15,29] and modifies Λ such that $\lambda_i := \lambda_i - \min_i \Lambda \ \forall i$. One main advantage of the classical shift eigenvalue correction is that if the smallest eigenvalue $\lambda_{\min}$ is already known, the operations can be accomplished with linear costs. In case $\lambda_{\min}$ is not yet available, at first, a determination or approximation procedure is needed to determine $\lambda_{\min}$, usually with higher computational costs. A spectrum shift enhances all the self-similarities and, therefore, the matrix's eigenvalues by the amount of λ_{min}, as shown in Fig. 2(e). During a shift correction, only the diagonal elements of the matrix are modified. Hence, there is no change of the similarity between any two different data points thus their relationships remain the same. However, this procedure may also increase the intrinsic dimensionality of the data space and introduce noise contributions. Eigenvalues without contribution zero contribution, respectively, receive a considerable boost - in particular, their new contribution level is $|\lambda_{min}|$ after the shift operation. If eigenvalues receive an increase in contribution during a correction procedure, their corresponding eigenvectors are considered important within the data. Thus, originally unimportant parts of the data are suddenly attributed a much higher significance.

2.4 Limitations

In the past, there have been various approaches to modify the eigenspectrum to ensure positive definiteness [41,51]. However, all these approaches suffer from certain limitations: Most approaches modify the eigenspectrum in a very aggressive way destroying large parts of its structure. In particular, the clip, flip, and square operator have an apparent strong impact. Additionally, they are also costly due to an involved cubic eigendecomposition accessing the eigenvalues. In general, the **clip** operator only *removes* eigenvalues, but generally keeps the majority of the eigenvalues unaffected. While this method is useful in case of negative eigenvalues induced by noise, it may also remove valuable contributions if these eigenvalues contain meaningful information. The flip operator, on the other hand, affects all negative eigenvalues by changing the sign and this will additionally lead to a reorganization of the eigenvalues. In the past, the **flip** operator has actually worked quite well in many scenarios and the information in the data has not been completely destroyed. Unfortunately, the necessity of an eigendecomposition makes the flip unattractive for practical applications. The **square** operator, in general, is similar to flip, but additionally emphasizes large eigencontributions while reducing eigenvalues smaller than one. The **classical shift** operator is only changing the diagonal of the similarity matrix leading to a shift of the whole eigenspectrum by the provided offset. While this simple approach seems to be very reasonable, it has the major drawback that *all* eigenvalues are shifted, which also affects small or even zero eigenvalue contributions. While zero eigenvalues have no contribution in the original similarity matrix, they are artificially upraised by the classical shift operator. This may introduce a large amount of noise in the eigenspectrum causing substantial problems for many learning algorithms, such as kernel machines. In addition, the intrinsic dimensionality of the data is increased artificially, resulting in an even more challenging problem.

3   Eigenvalue Modification via Nullspace Integrated Shifting

To overcome these challenges, we introduced an improved version of the classic shift referred to as *advanced shift*. In the following section, we discuss the advanced shift and particularly the benefits of the nullspace correction. Additionally to the work of [37], we provide an accurate alternative estimation of the smallest eigenvalue and also give a convenient option for an out-of-sample extension.

3.1   Advanced Shift Correction

The advanced shift method in [37] performed better mainly due to two aspects: (a) it preserves the advantages of the classical shift - in particular, the lower computational costs - and (b) it compensates the disadvantages, such as artificial noise and an increased intrinsic dimension. The problem of the artificial induced noisy contribution of the classic shift is addressed in the advanced shift by means of a nullspace correction. The aim of this nullspace correction step is to eliminate shifted eigenvalues with near to zero contributions in the original data.

Accordingly, the overall structure of the eigenspectrum is widely kept by preserving eigenvalues with large absolute contribution and by keeping small values close to zero. All eigenvalues are positive after the correction step. We call this a *structure preserving encoding*. The procedure is summarized in Algorithm 1.

Algorithm 1. Advanced shift eigenvalue correction.

   Advanced_shift(S, k)
   if approximate to low-rank **then**
      $S := \text{LowRankApproximation}(S, k)$
   end if
   $\lambda := |\text{ShiftParameterDetermination}(S)|$
   $\mathbf{B} := \text{NullSpace}(S)$
   $\mathbf{N} := \mathbf{B} \cdot \mathbf{B}'$
   $S^* := S + 2 \cdot \lambda \cdot (I - \mathbf{N})$
   return S^*

As a first step in this algorithm, we suggest a low-rank approximation on the input similarity matrix S to map all small eigenvalues to exact zero. Although this may lead to loss of information, we assume that the near-zero eigenvalues actually arise from noise and are meaningless in the original data, compared to the preserved larger eigenvalues. This step is particular useful if the matrix has a large rank with many small, but non-vanishing eigenvalues. For a matrix with full rank, the advanced shift behaves similar to a classic shift with a doubled shift factor.

The low-rank approximation can be achieved by a restricted singular value decomposition with computational costs of $O(N^2)$. If the number of samples $N \leq 1000$, then the target rank was specified as $k = 30$ and $k = 100$, otherwise. The effect of such a low-rank approximation on the eigenvalues is shown in Fig. 3.

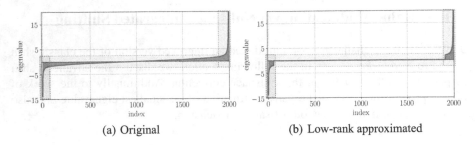

(a) Original   (b) Low-rank approximated

Fig. 3. Eigenspectrum plots of the Zongker dataset [26] used in the experiments in Sect. 4.1. Figure 3(a) shows the original spectrum of the eigenvalues of this dataset. Figure 3(b) shows the eigenspectrum after the low-rank approximation. The eigenvalues close to zero have lost their contribution after the approximation. (Color figure online)

Prior to the low-rank approximation, the eigenvalues in the orange shaded areas, Fig. 3, are close to zero, but not exactly zero, i.e. they contribute to the eigenspectrum. However, after the low-rank approximation, there is no contribution of these eigenvalues since all values in this segment are set to exactly zero. Thus, only the meaningful eigenvalues (in the red and green shaded boxes, Figs. 3(a) and 3(b)) retain their contribution during further steps.

It is essential to find a suitable shift parameter λ_{min} in order to keep the modification of the eigenspectrum as small as possible, but large enough to avoid negative eigenvalues. An inappropriately large shift parameter may also lead to numerical scaling problems. To determine a reliable shift parameter λ, various methods are available as we will discuss in Sect. 3.2 in more detail. In this paper we used a modified variant of the *von Mises* or power iteration [36] to get the smallest eigenvalue. After the determination, we take the absolute value of λ_{min} in the subsequent steps.

After the *ShiftParameterDetermination(S)*, the basis $\mathbf{B}$ of the nullspace is calculated. This can again be done in a cost-saving way by a restricted SVD, hence the computational costs remain at $O(N^2)$. Here, $\mathbf{B}$ consists of all vectors that form the basis for the nullspace of S, in other words all vectors mapping $\mathbf{S}$ to zero, such that $\mathbf{S} \cdot \mathbf{B} = 0$, where $\mathbf{B}$ is explicitly not zero.

The dimension of the nullspace can be obtained by the rank-nullity-theorem []. The rank-nullity-theorem states that the dimension of the nullspace equals the difference between the number of columns in S and the rank of S. At this point the importance of the low-rank approximation becomes evident: in case of a matrix S with full rank, the dimension of the nullspace becomes zero and thus, $\mathbf{B}$ is empty. Therefore, we recommend the low-rank approximation at the beginning to ensure the nullspace is not left empty and the setting does not fall back to the classical shift with all associated problems. After this step, the nullspace matrix $\mathbf{N}$ is calculated as the dot product of $\mathbf{B}$ and $\mathbf{B}'$. The subtraction of $\mathbf{N}$ from the identity matrix I $(I - \mathbf{N})$ can be seen as a projection matrix onto the orthogonal complement of the vectors in the nullspace $\mathbf{B}$. The matrix $\mathbf{N}$ can be computed with costs of $O(N^2)$. With this step, not only diagonal elements are modified like in the classical shift but also non-diagonal elements are slightly affected. This results in a modification of all eigenvalues except those for which $\mathbf{S} \cdot \mathbf{B} = 0$.

To ensure the final matrix preserves the information encoded in the large *negative* eigenvalues, the shift-factor is doubled and integrated into the shift matrix. At last, this shift matrix $2 \cdot \lambda \cdot (I - N)$ is added to the original matrix S. The eigenvalues of the final eigenspectrum are all non-negative. Since all sub tasks can be achieved with computational costs of about $O(N^2)$, the entire procedure can be done with $O(N^2)$ operations.

In the experiments, we analyze the effect of this transformation method with and without a low-rank approximation and compare it to the aforementioned alternative methods. Nevertheless, we can already tell that the cost of performing the advanced shift is comparable to the costs of the classical shift with λ_{min} and significantly lower than that of the clip and flip methods.

3.2 Determination and Approximation of the Shift Parameter

As the advanced shift relies on the classical shift, one main advantage of this correction method is its simplicity. As mentioned in the previous Section, the overall computational costs of this method strongly depend on the costs to calculate the smallest eigenvalue λ_{min}. Hence, choosing an appropriate λ_{min} is a crucial step leading to a trade-off problem: methods of low computational costs may determine an imprecise, potentially inappropriate λ_{min} while methods with high computational costs make the advanced shift more costly. Performing an eigenvalue decomposition on the complete matrix to determine λ_{min} is accurate but in general unattractive due to its cubic costs. For this purpose, efficient approaches include for example applying a low-rank approximated eigendecomposition on the original data, working with a sufficiently large shift parameter, making a guess of the smallest eigenvalue, or analyzing the eigenspectrum of only a subsample of the original data [51]. In our approach, we suggest employing a power iteration method, in particular, the *von Mises* approach but slightly modified to get a more accurate determination of λ_{min}[36]. This modified procedure gives an accurate estimation of the overall smallest eigenvalue. The classic von Mises returns only the dominant eigenvalue, i.e. the eigenvalue with the absolute highest value, regardless of whether it is positive or negative. The modified von Mises provides both the largest positive and negative eigenvalue. The modified von Mises iteration is described in Algorithm 2.

Algorithm 2. *ShiftParameterDetermination(S)* - modified von Mises.

Modified_von_Mises_iteration(S)
$[u_{max}, \lambda_{max}] = ClassicalVonMises(S)$
$S = (S - \lambda_{max} * I)$
$[u_{tempMin}, \lambda_{tempMin}] = ClassicalVonMises(-S)$
$\lambda_{min} = -(\lambda_{tempMin} - \lambda_{max})$
if $\lambda_{max} < \lambda_{min}$ switch $\lambda_{min,max}$
return λ_{min}

The first step, is the application of a classical von Mises iteration to identify the largest eigenvalue λ_{max}. Subsequently, each element on the diagonal of S is reduced by

λ_{max}. Afterwards, another von Mises iteration is performed, this time with the negative S. This modification of the von Mises iteration determines both the largest and the smallest eigenvalue.

3.3 Out-of-Sample Extension for New Test Points

Correcting eigenvalues to use non-psd data often poses some difficulties when the models are tested with new data points [51]. In general, one would like to modify the training and test data in a consistent way. Ideally, the modification is done directly on the similarity function and not on the completely computed matrix S. However, in case of eigenvalue correction methods this is not applicable, so the new points have to be transformed differently into the modified space.

In this section, we propose an efficient way for such a transformation of a new data point x_t. The following steps summarize the out of sample extension used in our experimental setup:

1. Calculation of the similarity values between x_t and at least three data points from X as *anchor points* using the same unmodified similarity measure. We obtain a similarity representation s_t of x_t by calculating a reasonable number of pairwise similarities to the training data. For example, the support vectors of the obtained model.
2. Lookup of the similarity values for all anchor points using S.
3. Calculate the weights necessary to reconstruct s_t by trilateration using the anchor point similarity vectors
4. The weights are now applied to the anchor point similarities of S^* (the modified similarities) and we obtain a trilaterated s_t^*

3.4 Structure Preservation of the Eigenspectrum

As mentioned before structure preservation refers to retention of larger eigenvalue contributions. Hence, those parts of the eigenspectrum that need not to be corrected should be kept close to its original state. In particular, only negative eigenvalues are in scope, requiring a correction step. These operations should be non-aggressive, which we call structure preserving. As illustrated in the synthetic example in Fig. 2, the various correction methods modify the eigenspectrum in different degrees and some of them change the structure of the eigenspectrum fundamentally.

These modifications to the eigenvalues include various operations, like changing the sign of the eigenvalues, deleting, amplifying or shrinking of eigenvalue contributions, or a reorganization of eigenvalues and their respective eigenvectors.

Particularly these operations have severe effects on methods that consider only a few (dominating) eigenvalues.

Figure 4 illustrates the impact of each eigenvalue correction method on the properties of the eigenspectrum, in particular, the eigenvalues of the real-world Zongker dataset. For further detailed information on this dataset, see Sect. 4.1.

Here, the y-axis illustrates the contribution value (or impact) of the eigenvalue and the x-axis represents the index of the eigenvalue. The left column of Fig. 4 (Subfigures 4(a), 4(c), 4(e), 4(g), 4(i)) shows the eigenspectra without a low-rank approximation,

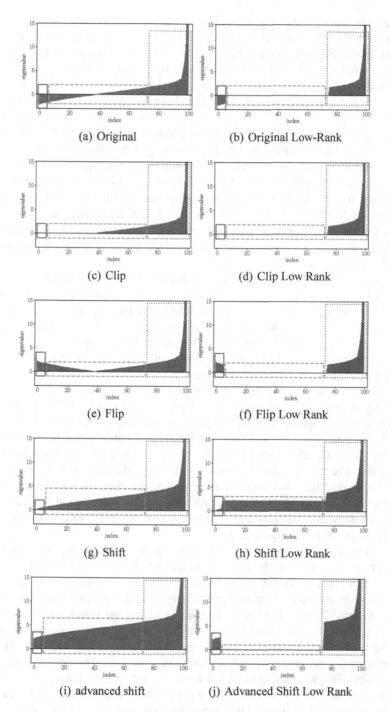

Fig. 4. Visualizations of the Zongker dataset's eigenspectra after applying various correction methods. Further details to this dataset are given in Sect. 4.1.

particularly in this case the original similarity matrix has full rank. The right column (Subfigures 4(b), 4(d), 4(f), 4(h), 4(j)) comprises the low-rank version of the eigenspectrum: In the following figures, the choice of color and linestyle of the highlighted regions is as follows: The red rectangle (solid line) highlights those negative parts of the eigenvalues which are negative in the original data and for which it is essential that their contribution is preserved in the data. The orange rectangle (dashed line) represents those eigenvalues that are close to zero or exactly zero. The green rectangle (dotted line) highlights those parts that contained the positive eigenvalues in the original data. Also, their contribution should also be kept unchanged in order not to manipulate the eigenspectrum too aggressive. Figure 4(a) illustrates the eigenspectrum of the original dataset without any modification. In this example, the eigenspectrum contains both positive and negative eigenvalues, hence the original data is indefinite. Figure 4(b) shows the low-rank representation of the original data of 4(a). Here, the major negative and major positive eigenvalues (red/solid and green/dotted rectangle) are still present, but many eigenvalues, that have been close to zero before, are set to exactly 0 (black/dashed rectangle) after the approximation step.

Figure 4(c) and Fig. 4(d) show the eigenvalues after applying the clip operator to the eigenvalues shown in Figs. 4(a) and 4(b). In both cases, the major positive eigenvalues (green/dotted rectangle) remain unaffected. However, the negative eigenvalues close to zero (parts of the orange/dashed rectangle in Figures) and in particular the major negative eigenvalues (red/solid rectangle) are all set to exactly 0. By using the clip operator, the contributions to the eigenspectrum of both major negative and slightly negative eigenvalues are completely eliminated.

In contrast to clipping, the flip corrector preserves the contribution of the negative and slightly negative eigenvalues, shown in Figs. 4(e) and 4(f). When using the flip corrector, only the negative sign of the eigenvalue is changed to positive; thus, only the diagonal of the matrix is changed and not the entire matrix. Since the square operator behaves almost analogously to the flip operator, it was not listed separately here. Squaring the values of a matrix significantly increases the impact of the major eigenvalues compared to the minor eigenvalues. This leads to a huge change in the respective eigenvalue's magnitude. If an essential part of the data's information is located in the small eigenvalues, this part gets a proportionally reduced contribution, against the significantly increased major eigenvalues.

The modified eigenspectra after applications of the classical shift operator are presented in Figs. 4(g) and 4(h): by increasing all eigenvalues of the spectrum, the higher negative eigenvalues (red/solid rectangle) that had more impact now only remain with zero or close to zero contribution. Furthermore, a higher contribution was assigned to those eigenvalues that previously had no or nearly no effect on the eigenspectrum (orange/dashed rectangle). As a result, the classical shift increases the number of non-zero eigencontributions by introducing artificial noise into the data. The same is also evident for the advanced shift without low-rank approximation depicted in Fig. 4(j). Since the Zongker dataset is of full rank, the nullspace is empty (Rank-Nullity-Theorem) and thus there is only a shift twice of the shift parameter on the diagonal. Here, the importance of a low rank approximation becomes evident, otherwise the advanced shift behaves analogously to the classical shift. As there are many eigenvalues close to zero but not exactly zero in this data set, all these eigenvalues are also increased in the advanced shift, but can be cured in the low-rank approach.

Unlike the advanced shift approach without low-rank approximation, depicted in Fig. 4(j), a low-rank representation of the data leads to a shifting of only those eigenvalues that had relevant contributions before (red/solid rectangle). Eigenvalues with previously almost zero contribution (orange/dashed rectangle), get a contribution of exactly zero by the approximation and are therefore not shifted in the advanced shift method.

In summary, the structure of the eigenspectrum is only preserved by using the flip corrector (including noise contributions), partially in the square operator, and also by the advanced shift operator with low-rank approximation but not the clip or the classic shift corrector. Although this section contained results exclusively for the Zongker dataset, we observed similar findings for other indefinite datasets as well. Our first findings show, that a more sophisticated treatment of the similarity matrix is needed to obtain a suitable psd matrix. This makes our method more appropriate compared to simpler approaches such as the classic shift or clip.

4 Experiments

This section contains a series of experiments highlighting the effectiveness of our approach in combination with a low-rank approximation. We evaluate the algorithm for a set of benchmark data that are typically used in the context of proximity-based supervised learning. The data are briefly described in the following and summarized in Table 2, with details given in the references. Subsequently, the experimental setup and the performance of the different eigenvalue correction methods on the benchmark datasets are presented and discussed in this section.

4.1 Datasets

We use a variety of standard benchmark data for similarity-based learning. All data sets used in this experimental setup are indefinite with different spectral properties. If the data are given as dissimilarities, a corresponding similarity matrix can be obtained by double centering [41]: $S = -JDJ/2$ with $J = (I - \mathbf{1}\mathbf{1}^\top/N)$, with identity matrix I and vector of ones $\mathbf{1}$.

The datasets used for the experiments are described in the following and summarized in Table 2, with details given in the references. The triplet (p, q, z) is also referred to as the signature. In this context, the signature describes the ratio of positive to negative and zero eigenvalues of the respective data set.

1. **Aural Sonar** consists of 100 signals with two classes, representing sonar signals dissimilarity measures to investigate the human ability to distinguish different types of sonar signals by ear. Details are provided in [7].
2. **Balls3d/Balls50d** consist of 200/2000 samples in two/four classes. The dissimilarities are generated between two constructed balls using the shortest distance on the surfaces. The original data description is provided in [42].
3. The **Catcortex** data set is provided as a 65×65 dissimilarity matrix describing the connection strengths between 65 cortical areas of a cat from four regions (classes): auditory (A), frontolimbic (F), somatosensory (S) and visual (V). The dissimilarity values are measured on an ordinal scale.

4. The Kopenhagen **Chromosomes** data set constitutes 4,200 human chromosomes from 21 classes represented by grey-valued images. These are transferred to strings measuring the thickness of their silhouettes. These strings are compared using edit distance. Details are provided in [39].
5. The **Delft gestures** (1500 points, 20 classes, balanced, signature: (963,536,1)), taken from [12], is a set of dissimilarities generated from a sign-language interpretation problem. It consists of 1500 points with 20 classes and 75 points per class. The gestures are measured by two video cameras observing the positions of the two hands in 75 repetitions of creating 20 different signs. The dissimilarities are computed using a dynamic time-warping procedure on the sequence of positions (Lichtenauer, Hendriks, Reinders 2008).

Table 2. Overview of the datasets used in our experimental setup. Details are given in the textual description.

Dataset	#samples	#classes	Signature
Aural Sonar	100	2	$(62,38,0)$
Balls3d	200	2	$(48,152,0)$
Balls50d	2000	4	$(853,1147,0)$
Catcortex	65	4	$(49,16,0)$
Chromosomes	4200	21	$(2258,1899,43)$
DelftGestures	1500	20	$(963,536,1)$
FaceRec	945	139	$(794,150,1)$
Flowcyto-1	612	3	$(538,73,1)$
Flowcyto-2	612	3	$(26,73,582)$
Flowcyto-3	612	3	$(541,70,1)$
Flowcyto-4	612	3	$(26,73,582)$
Gauss with overlap	1000	2	$(469,531,0)$
Gauss without overlap	1000	2	$(468,532,0)$
Patrol	241	8	$(233,8,0)$
Prodom	2604	53	$(1502,680,422)$
Protein	213	4	$(170,40,3)$
Sonatas	1068	5	$(1063,4,1)$
SwissProt	10988	10	$(8487,2500,1)$
Tox-21 (AllBit)	14484	2	$(2049,0,12435)$
Tox-21 (Assymetric)	14484	2	$(1888,3407,9189)$
Tox-21 (Kulczynski)	14484	2	$(2048,2048,10388)$
Tox-21 (McConnaughey)	14484	2	$(2048,2048,10388)$
Vibrio	1100	49	$(851,248,1)$
Voting	435	2	$(178,163,94)$
Zongker	2000	10	$(1039,961,0)$

6. **Facerec** dataset consists of 945 sample faces with 139 classes, representing sample faces of people, compared by the cosine similarity as measure. Details are provided in [7].

7. The **Flowcyto** dataset is based on 612 FL3-A DNA flowcytometer histograms from breast cancer tissues in 256 resolution. The initial data were acquired by M. Nap and N. van Rodijnen of the Atrium Medical Center in Heerlen, The Netherlands, during 2000–2004, using tubes 3, 4,5, and 6 of a DACO Galaxy flowcytometer. Overall, this data set consists of four datasets, each representing the same data, but with different proximity measure settings. Histograms are labeled in 3 classes: aneuploid (335 patients), diploid (131), and tetraploid (146). Dissimilarities between normalized histograms are computed using the L1 norm, correcting for possible different calibration factors [12]. Further information on the analysis of flow cytometry data in a more classical setting can be found in [5].

8. For working with **Gauss** data, we create two datasets X, each consisting of 1000 data points in two dimensions divided into two classes. Data of the first dataset are linearly separable, whereas data of the second dataset are overlapping. To calculate dissimilarity matrix D, we use $D = \tanh(-2.25 \cdot X \cdot X^T + 2)$.

9. The **Patrol** data set is about the classification of 241 people into one of 8 patrol units based on whom people claimed was in their unit when asked to name five people in their unit.

10. The **ProDom** dataset with signature (1502,680,422) consists of 2604 protein sequences with 53 labels. It contains a comprehensive set of protein families and appeared first in the work of [46]. The pairwise structural alignments were computed by [46]. Each sequence belongs to a group labeled by experts; here, we use the data as provided in [12].

11. **Protein:** the Protein data set has sequence-alignment similarities for 213 proteins and is used for comparing and classifying protein sequences according to its four classes of globins: heterogeneous globin (G), hemoglobin-A (HA), hemoglobin-B (HB) and myoglobin (M). The signature is (170,40,3), where class one through four contains 72, 72, 39, and 30 points, respectively [24].

12. **Sonatas** dataset consists of 1068 sonatas from five composers (classes) from two consecutive eras of western classical music. The musical pieces were taken from the online MIDI database *Kunst der Fuge* and transformed to similarities by normalized compression distance [38].

13. **SwissProt:** the SwissProt data set (SWISS), with a signature (8487, 2500, 1), consists of 10,988 points of protein sequences in 30 classes taken as a subset from the popular SwissProt database of protein sequences [6]. The considered subset of the SwissProt database refers to the release 37. A typical protein sequence consists of a string of amino acids, and the length of the full sequences varies between 30 to more than 1000 amino acids depending on the sequence. The ten most common classes such as Globin, Cytochrome b, Protein kinase st, etc. provided by the Prosite labeling [16] were taken, leading to 5,791 sequences. Due to this choice, an associated classification problem maps the sequences to their corresponding Prosite labels. These sequences are compared using Smith-Waterman which computes a local alignment of sequences [20]. This database is the standard source for

identifying and analyzing protein sequences such that an automated classification and processing technique would be very desirable.

14. **Tox-21:** The initial intention of the Tox-21 challenges is to predict whether certain chemical compounds have the potential to disrupt processes in the human body that may lead to adverse health effects, i. e. are toxic to humans [25]. This version of the dataset contains 14484 molecules encoded as Simplified Molecular Input Line Entry Specification (SMILE) codes. SMILE codes are ASCII-strings to encode complex chemical structures. For example, Lauryldiethanolamine has the molecular formula of $C_{16}H_{35}NO_2$ and is encoded as CCCCCCCCCC-CCN(CCO)CCO. Each smile code is described as a morgan fingerprint [14, 45] and encoded as a bit-vector with a length of 2048 via the RDKit[1] framework. The molecules are compared to each other by using the non-psd binary similarity metrics AllBit, Kulczynski, McConnaughey, and Asymmetric provided by the RDKIT. The similarity matrix is based on pairwise similarities calculated by the respective metric. According to the applied similarity metrics, the resulting matrices are varying in their amount of negative eigenvalues. The task of the dataset is binary classification, which is either toxic or non-toxic for every given molecule and should be predicted by a machine learning algorithm.

15. **Vibrio:** Bacteria of the genus Vibrio are Gram-negative, primarily facultative anaerobes, forming motile rods. Contact with contaminated water and the consumption of raw seafood are the primary infection factors for Vibrio-associated diseases. Vibrio parahaemolyticus, for instance, is one of the leading causes of foodborne gastroenteritis worldwide. The vibrio data set consists of 1,100 samples of vibrio bacteria populations characterized by mass spectra. The spectra encounter approximately 42,000 mass positions. The full data set consists of 49 classes of vibrio-sub-species. The mass spectra are preprocessed with a standard workflow using the BioTyper software [35]. As usual, mass spectra display strong functional characteristics due to the dependency of subsequent masses, such that problem-adapted similarities such as described in [4, 35] are beneficial. In our case, similarities are calculated using a specific similarity measure as provided by the BioTyper software [35] with a signature (851,248,1).

16. **Voting** contains 435 samples in 2 classes, representing categorical data, which are compared based on the value difference metric [7].

17. **Zongker** dataset is a digit dissimilarity dataset. The dissimilarity measure was computed between 2000 handwritten digits in 10 classes, with 200 entries in each class [26].

4.2   Results

We evaluate the accuracy of the proposed advanced shift correction on the mentioned datasets against other eigenvalue correction methods using the standard python SVC classifier from sklearn-package. As the data was already given as pairwise similarity matrices, we used 'precomputed' for the attribute *kernel* to restrict an additional kernel trick within the SVM implementation. We verified that the corrected input kernel matrix

---

[1] https://www.rdkit.org/.

was indeed psd by an additional test using an eigendecomposition, no fails were found. Again, this is typically important for kernel methods to guarantee the expected convergence of the optimization framework. Nevertheless, we also compare our approach in a setup without a correction, thus leaving the input matrix non-psd. As discussed in [21], it may nevertheless lead to good results. For a better evaluation of the considered methods, the low-rank approximation was applied to all eigenvalue correction methods. Only when employing the original data in the SVM, the low-rank approximation was omitted to ensure that no negative parts are lost. Once again, please note that the simple application of a low-rank approximation only does not lead to the intended results. If the negative eigenvalues are particularly small, a low-rank approximation can eliminate these eigenvalues, but this is rarely the case. Accordingly, convergence problems and information loss as well as inadequate models may still occur due to the negative eigenvalues in uncorrected input data.

For the evaluation of the experiments, we stored the algorithm's accuracy and its standard deviation achieved in a ten-fold cross-validation shown in Table 3. Additionally, we track the percentage of support vectors as an indicator of the model complexity. The results for the percentage of necessary support vectors are shown in Table 4.

The parameter C of the SVM has been selected for each correction method by a grid search on independent data not used during this evaluation phase. We ran the entire experiments at least three times for each benchmark dataset. Some datasets are already

Table 3. Prediction accuracy (mean ± standard-deviation) for the various data sets and methods in comparison to the advanced shift method.

Dataset	Adv. shift	Original	Classic shift	Clip	Flip	Square
Aural Sonar	88.0 ± 0.13	88.0 ± 8.72	**89.0 ± 0.08**	86.0 ± 0.11	88.0 ± 0.06	87.0 ± 0.11
Balls3d	**100.0 ± 0.0**	59.5 ± 9.6	37.0 ± 0.07	78.5 ± 0.05	96.0 ± 0.04	55.0 ± 0.09
Balls50d	**48.15 ± 0.04**	25.4 ± 2.27	20.65 ± 0.02	27.2 ± 0.04	41.15 ± 0.03	25.05 ± 0.02
Catcortex	87.86 ± 10.93	85.24 ± 13.38	92.62 ± 9.79	89.52 ± 14.53	95.0 ± 7.64	**95.48 ± 6.94**
Chromosomes	96.45 ± 0.01	n. c	n. c	38.95 ± 0.02	**97.29 ± 0.0**	96.07 ± 0.01
Delft Gestures	98.07 ± 1.01	97.87 ± 0.72	96.8 ± 1.29	**98.2 ± 0.9**	98.07 ± 1.05	97.6 ± 1.2
FaceRec	62.33 ± 0.05	85.92 ± 2.44	62.22 ± 0.07	61.92 ± 0.07	63.27 ± 0.05	**86.13 ± 0.02**
Flowcyto-1	69.28 ± 5.10	63.74 ± 6.50	66.02 ± 5.45	69.93 ± 6.31	70.26 ± 5.41	**70.58 ± 6.09**
Flowcyto-2	**72.4 ± 5.85**	62.09 ± 5.36	65.69 ± 6.44	71.39 ± 4.96	70.42 ± 3.84	71.08 ± 2.86
Flowcyto-3	70.26 ± 3.58	62.09 ± 0.44	64.55 ± 5.61	70.74 ± 5.70	**71.10 ± 4.67**	70.75 ± 3.03
Flowcyto-4	70.43 ± 6.12	59.88 ± 0.58	63.54 ± 6.97	**71.10 ± 4.92**	70.25 ± 5.31	68.29 ± 5.68
Gauss with overlap	**91.6 ± 0.03**	1.5 ± 1.2	64.55 ± 5.61	70.74 ± 5.70	−71.10 ± 4.67}	70.75 ± 3.03
Gauss without overlap	**100.0 ± 0.0**	15.4 ± 3.88	2.2 ± 0.01	99.7 ± 0.0	**100.0 ± 0.0**	**100.0 ± 0.0**
Patrol	**26.15 ± 10.73**	20.78 ± 6.52	23.65 ± 7.68	24.45 ± 9.47	22.78 ± 7.09	23.67 ± 8.17
Prodom	**99.85 ± 0.25**	n. c	99.77 ± 0.26	99.77 ± 0.31	99.77 ± 0.25	99.65 ± 0.47
Protein	**99.07 ± 0.02**	59.63 ± 5.98	58.31 ± 0.09	98.59 ± 0.02	99.05 ± 0.02	98.61 ± 0.02
Sonatas	**94.29 ± 0.02**	87.55 ± 2.38	90.73 ± 0.02	93.64 ± 0.04	94.19 ± 0.02	93.44 ± 0.03
SwissProt	**97.55 ± 0.01**	97.48 ± 0.5	96.48 ± 0.0	96.42 ± 0.0	96.54 ± 0.0	97.43 ± 0.0
Tox-21 (AllBit)	97.36 ± 0.49	97.37 ± 0.47	**97.38 ± 0.44**	97.33 ± 0.52	**97.38 ± 0.30**	97.35 ± 0.38
Tox-21 (Assymetric)	**97.46 ± 0.44**	90.40 ± 2.01	95.28 ± 0.64	96.96 ± 0.46	97.33 ± 0.35	97.18 ± 0.48
Tox-21 (Kulczynski)	**97.36 ± 0.39**	92.81 ± 2.16	95.28 ± 0.54	97.20 ± 0.26	97.29 ± 0.37	97.30 ± 0.31
Tox-21 (McConnaughey)	**97.34 ± 0.41**	92.08 ± 2.02	94.97 ± 0.56	97.15 ± 0.50	97.33 ± 0.32	97.15 ± 0.54
Vibrio	**100.0 ± 0.00**	**100.0 ± 0.00**	**100.0 ± 0.00**	**100.0 ± 0.00**	**100.0 ± 0.00**	**100.0 ± 0.00**
Voting	**97.24 ± 0.03**	96.33 ± 2.53	95.88 ± 0.03	96.59 ± 0.04	96.77 ± 0.03	96.77 ± 0.02
Zongker	**97.7 ± 0.01**	92.05 ± 1.01	92.85 ± 0.01	96.85 ± 0.01	97.2 ± 0.01	96.75 ± 0.01

identified as showing convergence problems when working with kernel methods [37, 51]. In our experiments, convergence issues mainly occurred in the Chromosomes and Prodom datasets with the original non-psd data and with the classic shift (not converged - subsequently n.c.).

In Table 3, we show the classification accuracy for the experimental setup consisting of the considered datasets and various eigenvalue correction methods.

Using uncorrected data (column labeled: original) reliable results were obtained rarely compared with other classical correction methods. Therefore, we assume that a correction step is indeed necessary since the use of uncorrected non-psd data shows clear limitations in accuracy. In summary, the presented advanced shift combined with the modified von Mises iteration performed best, followed by the flip correction method and the square correction method. It becomes evident how important the preservation of the eigenspectrum's structure is for the performance in supervised learning tasks: advanced shift, Flip and Square are all capable of preserving the structure of the eigenspectrum (in case of the square method at least roughly), since the dominant eigenvalues both positive and negative are retained by means of these methods. As the low-rank approximation leads to a large number of truly zero eigenvalues, the noisy contributions were removed from the data. Especially, the advanced shift benefits from the elimination of the small eigenvalues, as seen in [37], where the low-rank approximation led to a boost in performance. Also, the eigenvalue clip provides considerable results in the experiments and is only slightly behind Flip, Square and advanced shift. The classical shift, which has been frequently recommended in the literature, fell significantly behind the other methods in our experiments. The plain choice of a sufficiently high shifting factor λ_{min} solves the metric problems, but seems to disturb the eigenstructure.

Additionally to the accuracy of the considered methods, the number of support vectors of each trained SVM model was gathered as an indication for the model's complexity. The results are shown in Table 4 in terms of the percentage of necessary support vectors.

For this purpose, the number of points that serve as support vectors is set in relation to the total number of data points. The higher this percentage, the more data points are needed for a successful model. This also implies, however, higher complexity of the model, which often results in a reduced generalization to new data points and additional costs in the out of sample extension. In summary, the results shown in Table 4 highlight the comparability of the advanced shift to the other approaches. In general, compared to the original SVM using uncorrected non-psd data without a low-rank approximation, the advanced shift performed better almost consistently and in some cases even significantly. Furthermore, compared to the classic shift correction, the advanced shift is significantly better in accuracy and the percentage of required support vectors. Considering the complexity in terms of required support vectors, the advanced shift performs competitively compared to clip and flip. However, in relation to the square correction method, the advanced shift suffers from minor limitations.

In summary, the advanced shift is competitive to the clipping and flipping correction methods but generally requires a higher number of support vectors compared to the square correction. Considering the accuracy as well as the number of necessary support vectors and the computational costs, the advanced shift is preferable to clip and flip

Table 4. Percentage of data points that are necessary for the model (in terms of support vectors) to build a well-fitting decision hyperplane.

Dataset	Adv. shift	Original	Classic shift	Clip	Flip	Square
Aural Sonar	53.1%	74.5%	86.7%	76.8%	77.3%	**42.4%**
Bacteria	**44.0%**	98.8%	62.4%	46.6%	47.1%	44.4%
Balls3d	**17.4%**	51.8%	100.0%	56.6%	48.6%	19.1%
Balls50d	**60.8%**	94.7%	96.3%	95.2%	95.7%	94.9%
Catcortex	77.0%	67.2%	92.7%	61.9%	65.4%	**53.9%**
Chromosomes	39.3%	n. c	n. c	30.3%	30.6%	**23.8%**
Delft Gestures	76.0%	72.3%	100.0%	58.3%	58.2%	**29.1%**
FaceRec	90.5%	91.5%	90.5%	90.5%	90.5%	**64.1%**
Flowcyto-1	**60.9%**	64.8%	99.7%	61.6%	63.6%	62.4%
Flowcyto-2	58.7%	72.6%	96.7%	**56.9%**	58.1%	57.7%
Flowcyto-3	57.7%	63.0%	99.3%	**56.7%**	57.4%	58.6%
Flowcyto-4	**58.9%**	69.0%	99.6%	59.3%	**58.8%**	61.8%
Gauss with overlap	9.2%	99.0%	99.0%	3.5%	5.9%	**2.2%**
Gauss without overlap	24.4%	84.8%	95.7%	34.0%	21.1%	**21.0%**
Patrol	99.7%	99.7%	99.7%	99.7%	99.7%	99.7%
Prodom	18.7%	n. c	18.7%	18.7%	18.8%	**12.9%**
Protein	38.6%	80.3%	99.8%	21.5%	21.5%	**12.9%**
Sonatas	38.2%	67.8%	78.7%	34.5%	34.5%	**26.9%**
SwissProt	13.9%	48.9%	13.9%	13.9%	13.9%	**12.2%**
Tox-21 (AllBit)	5.5%	5.8%	7.4%	6.5%	7.2%	**4.6%**
Tox-21 (Assymetric)	5.4%	7.3%	10.0%	7.6%	7.1%	**4.6%**
Tox-21 (Kulczynski)	5.9%	8.0%	10.0%	7.2%	7.1%	**5.3%**
Tox-21 (McConnaughey)	5.6%	8.4%	8.3%	7.6%	7.5%	**4.2%**
Vibrio	99.6%	100.0%	99.6%	99.6%	99.6%	**92.0%**
Voting	9.7%	8.6%	26.2%	**8.5%**	**8.5%**	9.1%
Zongker	50.4%	63.5%	100.0%	31.5%	34.5%	**22.5%**

and comparable to the square correction. As already noted in previous studies, there is no simple solution for eigenvalue correction methods on non-metric data. Therefore, we introduced an efficient way for non-psd data to be handled in common methods like kernel machines. Nevertheless, when analyzing non-psd data, various aspects of the data always need to be considered, especially the relevance of the negative portions. The results in this section clearly show that the advanced shift works particularly well when the negative eigenvalues possess a considerable contribution to the eigenspectrum. Additionally, due to the low-rank approximation as preprocessing step, the structure of the eigenvalues is preserved.

5 Conclusions

In this paper, we discussed a recently proposed eigenvalue correction method for non-metric proximity data, referred to as *advanced shift*. In particular, we highlighted how indefinite data is transformed into positive semi-definiteness while simultaneously preserving large parts of the eigenspectrum. Standard correction methods and their impact on the eigenspectrum were shown as well as their major limitations, advantages and disadvantages. Surprisingly, the classic shift correction is frequently recommended in the literature suggesting the simple application of a sufficiently high offset to cure the indefiniteness problems. The associated destruction of the eigenspectrum due to shifting all eigenvalues - including those with small or zero contribution - is frequently neglected.

Contrary to this, as a result of our approach, the overall structure of the eigenvalues is preserved: eigenvalues with vanishing contribution before the shift remain irrelevant after the shift as well as eigenvalues with a high contribution keep high relevance after the correction. Moreover, the advanced shift performed superior to many other methods not only in terms of retaining the eigenspectrum, but also in our experimental setup. We analyzed the effectiveness of the advanced shift on a broad spectrum of classification problems from indefinite learning. In combination with the low-rank approximation, our approach performed competitive, in most cases considerable better compared to other methods.

In future work, further matrix approximation techniques will be analyzed together with the advanced shift. Also unsupervised learning tasks are of interest as further research.

Acknowledgments. At first, we would like to thank Michael Biehl (University of Groningen) for useful discussions, proofreading and supporting work in the initial conference publication [37]. We also thank Gaelle Bonnet-Loosli for providing support with indefinite learning and R. Duin, Delft University for various support with DisTools and PRTools[12]. We would like to thank Dr. Markus Kostrzewa and Dr. Thomas Maier for providing the Vibrio data set and expertise regarding the biotyping approach and Dr. Katrin Sparbier for discussions about the SwissProt data (all Bruker Corp.).

A related conference publication by the same authors was published at the 9th International Conference on Pattern Recognition Applications and Method (ICPRAM2020) (see [37]) - copyright related material is not affected.

References

1. Alabdulmohsin, I.M., Cissé, M., Gao, X., Zhang, X.: Large margin classification with indefinite similarities. Mach. Learn. **103**(2), 215–237 (2016)
2. Azizov, T.Y., Iokhvidov, I.S.: Linear operators in spaces with indefinite metric and their applications. J. Sov. Math. **15**, 438–490 (1981)
3. Balcan, M.F., Blum, A., Srebro, N.: A theory of learning with similarity functions. Mach. Learn. **72**(1–2), 89–112 (2008)
4. Barbuddhe, S.B., et al.: Rapid identification and typing of listeria species by matrix-assisted laser desorption ionization-time of flight mass spectrometry. Appl. Environ. Microbiol. **74**(17), 5402–5407 (2008)

5. Biehl, M., Bunte, K., Schneider, P.: Analysis of flow cytometry data by matrix relevance learning vector quantization. PLoS One **8**, e59401 (2013)
6. Boeckmann, B., et al.: The SWISS-PROT protein knowledgebase and its supplement TrEMBL in 2003. Nucleic Acids Res. **31**, 365–370 (2003)
7. Chen, H., Tino, P., Yao, X.: Probabilistic classification vector machines. IEEE Trans. Neural Netw. **20**(6), 901–914 (2009)
8. Chen, Y., Garcia, E., Gupta, M., Rahimi, A., Cazzanti, L.: Similarity-based classification: concepts and algorithms. J. Mach. Learn. Res. **10**, 747–776 (2009)
9. Cichocki, A., Amari, S.I.: Families of alpha- beta- and gamma-divergences: flexible and robust measures of similarities. Entropy **12**(6), 1532–1568 (2010)
10. Cilibrasi, R., Vitányi, P.M.B.: Clustering by compression. IEEE Trans. Inf. Theory **51**(4), 1523–1545 (2005)
11. Dubuisson, M.P., Jain, A.: A modified hausdorff distance for object matching. In: Proceedings of the 12th IAPR International Conference on Pattern Recognition, Conference A: Computer Vision & Image Processing, vol. 1, pp. 566–568, October 1994
12. Duin, R.P.: PRTools, March 2012. http://www.prtools.org
13. Duin, R.P.W., Pękalska, E.: Non-euclidean dissimilarities: causes and informativeness. In: Hancock, E.R., Wilson, R.C., Windeatt, T., Ulusoy, I., Escolano, F. (eds.) SSPR /SPR 2010. LNCS, vol. 6218, pp. 324–333. Springer, Heidelberg (2010). https://doi.org/10.1007/978-3-642-14980-1_31
14. Figueras, J.: Morgan revisited. J. Chem. Inf. Comput. Sci. **33**, 717–718 (1993)
15. Filippone, M.: Dealing with non-metric dissimilarities in fuzzy central clustering algorithms. Int. J. Approx. Reasoning **50**(2), 363–384 (2009)
16. Gasteiger, E., Gattiker, A., Hoogland, C., Ivanyi, I., Appel, R., Bairoch, A.: ExPASy: the proteomics server for in-depth protein knowledge and analysis. Nucleic Acids Res. **31**, 3784–3788 (2003)
17. Gisbrecht, A., Schleif, F.: Metric and non-metric proximity transformations at linear costs. Neurocomputing **167**, 643–657 (2015)
18. Goodfellow, I.J., Bengio, Y., Courville, A.: Deep Learning. MIT Press, Cambridge (2016)
19. Graepel, T., Obermayer, K.: A stochastic self-organizing map for proximity data. Neural Comput. **11**(1), 139–155 (1999)
20. Gusfield, D.: Algorithms on Strings, Trees, and Sequences: Computer Science and Computational Biology. Cambridge University Press, Cambridge (1997)
21. Haasdonk, B.: Feature space interpretation of SVMs with indefinite kernels. IEEE TPAMI **27**(4), 482–492 (2005)
22. Harol, A., Pękalska, E., Verzakov, S., Duin, R.P.W.: Augmented embedding of dissimilarity data into (pseudo-)euclidean spaces. In: Yeung, D.-Y., Kwok, J.T., Fred, A., Roli, F., de Ridder, D. (eds.) SSPR /SPR 2006. LNCS, vol. 4109, pp. 613–621. Springer, Heidelberg (2006). https://doi.org/10.1007/11815921_67
23. Higham, N.: Computing a nearest symmetric positive semidefinite matrix. Linear Algebra Appl. **103**(C), 103–118 (1988)
24. Hofmann, T., Buhmann, J.M.: Pairwise data clustering by deterministic annealing. IEEE Trans. Pattern Anal. Mach. Intell. **19**(1), 1–14 (1997)
25. Huang, R., et al.: Tox21challenge to build predictive models of nuclear receptor and stress response pathways as mediated by exposure to environmental chemicals and drugs. Front. Environ. Sci. **3**, 85 (2016)
26. Jain, A., Zongker, D.: Representation and recognition of handwritten digits using deformable templates. IEEE TPAMI **19**(12), 1386–1391 (1997)
27. Kar, P., Jain, P.: Supervised learning with similarity functions. In: Proceedings of Advances in Neural Information Processing Systems, 26th Annual Conference on Neural Information Processing Systems, Lake Tahoe, Nevada, United States, vol. 25, pp. 215–223 (2012)

28. Kohonen, T., Somervuo, P.: How to make large self-organizing maps for nonvectorial data. Neural Netw. **15**(8–9), 945–952 (2002)
29. Laub, J.: Non-metric pairwise proximity data. Ph.D. thesis, TU Berlin (2004)
30. Lee, J., Verleysen, M.: Generalizations of the Lp norm for time series and its application to self-organizing maps. In: Cottrell, M. (ed.) 5th Workshop on Self-Organizing Maps, vol. 1, pp. 733–740 (2005)
31. Ling, H., Jacobs, D.W.: Using the inner-distance for classification of articulated shapes. In: CVPR 2005, San Diego, CA, USA, pp. 719–726. IEEE Computer Society (2005)
32. Loosli, G.: TrIK-SVM: an alternative decomposition for kernel methods in Krein spaces. In: Verleysen, M. (ed.) In Proceedings of the 27th European Symposium on Artificial Neural Networks (ESANN) 2019, pp. 79–94. d-side publications, Evere (2019)
33. Loosli, G., Canu, S., Ong, C.S.: Learning SVM in Krein spaces. IEEE Trans. Pattern Anal. Mach. Intell. **38**(6), 1204–1216 (2016)
34. Luss, R., d'Aspremont, A.: Support vector machine classification with indefinite kernels. Math. Program. Comput. **1**(2–3), 97–118 (2009)
35. Maier, T., Klebel, S., Renner, U., Kostrzewa, M.: Fast and reliable MALDI-TOF MS-based microorganism identification. Nature Methods **3**, 1–2 (2006)
36. Mises, R.V., Pollaczek-Geiringer, H.: Praktische verfahren der gleichungsaufloesung. ZAMM - J. Appl. Math. Mech. / Zeitschrift für Angewandte Mathematik und Mechanik **9**(2), 152–164 (1929)
37. Münch, M., Raab., C., Biehl., M., Schleif., F.: Structure preserving encoding of non-euclidean similarity data. In: Proceedings of the 9th International Conference on Pattern Recognition Applications and Methods, ICPRAM, vol. 1, pp. 43–51. INSTICC, SciTePress (2020)
38. Mokbel, B.: Dissimilarity-based learning for complex data. Ph.D. thesis, University of Bielefeld (2016)
39. Neuhaus, M., Bunke, H.: Edit distance based kernel functions for structural pattern classification. Pattern Recogn. **39**(10), 1852–1863 (2006)
40. Oglic, D., Gärtner, T.: Scalable learning in reproducing kernel Krein spaces. In: Proceedings of the 36th International Conference on Machine Learning, ICML 2019, 9–15 June 2019, Long Beach, California, USA, pp. 4912–4921 (2019)
41. Pekalska, E., Duin, R.: The Dissimilarity Representation for Pattern Recognition. World Scientific, Singapore (2005)
42. Pękalska, E., Harol, A., Duin, R.P.W., Spillmann, B., Bunke, H.: Non-euclidean or non-metric measures can be informative. In: Yeung, D.-Y., Kwok, J.T., Fred, A., Roli, F., de Ridder, D. (eds.) SSPR /SPR 2006. LNCS, vol. 4109, pp. 871–880. Springer, Heidelberg (2006). https://doi.org/10.1007/11815921_96
43. Pekalska, E., Paclík, P., Duin, R.P.W.: A generalized kernel approach to dissimilarity-based classification. J. Mach. Learn. Res. **2**, 175–211 (2001)
44. Platt, J.C.: Fast training of support vector machines using sequential minimal optimization. In: Advances in Kernel Methods: Support Vector Learning, pp. 185–208. MIT Press, Cambridge (1999)
45. Ralaivola, L., Swamidass, S.J., Saigo, H., Baldi, P.: Graph kernels for chemical informatics. Neural Netw. **18**(8), 1093–1110 (2005)
46. Roth, V., Laub, J., Buhmann, J.M., Müller, K.R.: Going metric: denoising pairwise data. In: NIPS, pp. 817–824 (2002)
47. Sakoe, H., Chiba, S.: Dynamic programming algorithm optimization for spoken word recognition. IEEE Trans. Signal Process. **26**(1), 43–49 (1978)
48. Saralajew, S., Villmann, T.: Adaptive tangent distances in generalized learning vector quantization for transformation and distortion invariant classification learning. In: IJCNN 2016, Vancouver, BC, Canada, 2016, pp. 2672–2679 (2016)

49. Scheirer, W.J., Wilber, M.J., Eckmann, M., Boult, T.E.: Good recognition is non-metric. Pattern Recogn. **47**(8), 2721–2731 (2014)
50. Schleif, F., Raab, C., Tiño, P.: Sparsification of core set models in non-metric supervised learning. Pattern Recognit. Lett. **129**, 1–7 (2020)
51. Schleif, F., Tiño, P.: Indefinite proximity learning: a review. Neural Comput. **27**(10), 2039–2096 (2015)
52. Schleif, F., Tiño, P.: Indefinite core vector machine. Pattern Recogn. **71**, 187–195 (2017)
53. Shawe-Taylor, J., Cristianini, N.: Kernel Methods for Pattern Analysis and Discovery. Cambridge University Press, Cambridge (2004)
54. Sidiropoulos, A., et al.: Approximation algorithms for low-distortion embeddings into low-dimensional spaces. SIAM J. Discret. Math. **33**(1), 454–473 (2019)
55. Strassen, V.: Gaussian elimination is not optimal. Numerische Mathematik **13**(4), 354–356 (1969)
56. Yanardag, P., Vishwanathan, S.V.N.: Deep graph kernels. In: Proceedings of the 21th ACM SIGKDD International Conference on Knowledge Discovery and Data Mining, Sydney, NSW, Australia, 10–13 August 2015, pp. 1365–1374. ACM (2015)
57. Zhang, J., Zhu, M., Qian, Y.: protein2vec: predicting protein-protein interactions based on LSTM. IEEE/ACM Trans. Comput. Biol. Bioinf. 1 (2020)

Author Index

Printed in the United States
By Bookmasters